Rise of the Fit Pros

Create More Income, Influence, Impact, and
Independence Through In-Person & Online
Personal Training

Chris and Eric Martinez

First Edition 2020

Printed in the United States of America

Published by:

Dynamic Inner Circle

PO Box 34-1036
Los Angeles, CA 90034

www.Dynamicinnercircle.com

For more information about Chris and Eric Martinez or to book them for your next event, speaking engagement, podcast or media interview please visit:
www.chrisericmartinez.com/speaking

This book is dedicated to the people who have blessed our lives and helped us unlock our true potential:

Our courageous mother, Maria Martinez, and awesome older brother, Mike, who we look up to so much.
Chris's beautiful and supportive fiancé, Lissette.
Our friends back home in Santa Rosa and our friends here in Los Angeles who have supported us through thick and thin.
Our DIC (Dynamic Inner Circle) community and students, who we learn so much from every day.
Our mentors and coaches (Tai Lopez, Cole Hatter, Mark Lack, Sue B Zimmerman, Christopher Kai, Mike Arce, Rory Carruthers, Chris Mueller, Adam Felske, Jesse Navarro, Jonathon Kendall, and Michael Zeller) for always pushing us and leading by example.

Everyone who has enriched our lives, you know who you are, thank you!

Contents

Foreword

Fact: Online personal training is rapidly overtaking traditional, in-house personal training. Are you prepared? Building a successful online personal training business begins right here with *Rise of the Fit Pros*, by The Dynamic Duo, Chris and Eric Martinez. These guys are extremely knowledgeable coaches and very tactical in their approach to capitalizing on this new era in fitness.

I've been in the fitness industry for well over a decade. It's always been a passion of mine. In fact, I started out as a personal trainer and leader for some of the biggest fitness organizations in the industry—helping places like LA Fitness, Fitness One, Pure Fitness, and Gold's Gym build their personal training departments. I've seen first-hand the evolution of this industry. However, this shift to online training is nothing short of astonishing.

As the CEO of Loud Rumor, the #1 Agency in Fitness, I've dedicated my life to growing the fitness industry from individual personal trainers and large-scale personal training businesses to boutique fitness studios and franchises, and I've been keeping a close eye on this.

With the prevalence of the internet, online personal training is quickly becoming the preferred way to do business. As Chris and Eric brilliantly explain in this book, online personal training is a massive WIN-WIN for both trainers AND clients.

Trainers: Online trainers have the ability to make more money by taking on more clients while enjoying the freedom to control and scale their time. How does this benefit their clients?

Clients: Clients, too, have the freedom to workout wherever they want and, because their trainer has more flexibility, personal training costs are much lower...which clients love!

On average, in-house personal trainers make between $50-65 per hour. It sounds pretty decent on paper, until it becomes obvious that booking back-to-back sessions forty hours per week, Monday-Friday, 8am-5pm is impossible. But, it's even worse than that...

Traditional, in-house personal training requires long, odd hours to accommodate client schedules. Speaking of schedules, paid-time-off doesn't exist. Trips are expensive and any time off is not only lost income but potentially a lost client.

One concern I've heard in the industry with transitioning into online personal training is client accountability. Many trainers fear they won't be able to help their clients hit goals and succeed because they can't hold them accountable. *Rise of the Fit Pros* proves why this actually isn't a concern with today's clients.

When I was a personal trainer, I would typically train a client three times a week for an hour per session. That's only three hours each week. So, I'm still trusting the client to follow through and do what it takes to hit their goals for 157 hours every week on their own.

Here's the truth: Clients only care about one thing: THE ANSWER. That's it.

They want to know what they have to do to achieve the results they want to achieve. What should they eat? What workouts should they do? How many times per week? Should they take supplements? In today's world, clients reverse engineer this process.

Clients used to hire a personal trainer first, then ask these questions second. Today, they Google these questions first, and find a personal trainer second. So, if you want to make more money, you need to be the answer their Google search comes up with. You're no longer the source, you're the search result. To win, you need to be the BEST search result.

With the knowledge and training in this book, Chris and Eric teach you how to become the BEST search result. That's just the beginning though. How do you turn someone finding you from a Google search into a paying online client?

You need a system. *Rise of the Fit Pros* dives deep into systems and processes. If you don't have a system in place, like most businesses, but especially with an online personal training business, you'll find yourself working way more hours than necessary to service your clients.

When this happens, you won't feel comfortable with the amount of income you're earning for the amount of hours you're putting in. You'll end up either (A) raising your prices, which could result in a loss of earned business, or (B) you'll want to go back to being an in-house personal trainer where you felt comfortable.

In my experience working with 2,000+ fitness studios and thousands of personal trainers all over the world, the most successful people running online training programs do so by building great systems. Not only to attract prospective clients, but also to get those clients to understand the program, appreciate the program, want to buy into the program, and to follow the program the way it's meant to be followed. The client knows the rules of communication and inputting information, so the online trainer can actually help the client hit fitness goals.

Very few people in the fitness industry (if ANY, for that matter) can explain this better than Chris and Eric Martinez. Chris and Eric really understand and appreciate processes and systems. They've taken the time to understand exactly what it takes to become a successful online personal trainer while understanding the importance of client success as well.

I've known Chris and Eric for about four years now. I first met these guys at a paid mastermind event ($2,500 just to be there) where we learned marketing-specific systems and processes. As I got to know them better, I realized that this wasn't the only time they spent money on coaching. In fact, they make it a regular practice to invest in regular coaching, masterminds, conferences, seminars, events, books, and podcasts in order to constantly improve and evolve their business.

As someone who loves to invest in great coaching, this is extremely important to me. If my coach doesn't have a great mentor, then in my mind, "It's only a matter of time before I surpass them." But, if my coach is constantly being mentored and seeking new opportunities to learn, then I know I have a coach who I'll continuously learn from. That's Chris and Eric.

After thoroughly reading through *Rise of the Fit Pros,* what Chris and Eric put together here is powerful. Whether you're a personal trainer in an early transition into online training or a personal trainer who's been dabbling in online training for a while, picking this book up now will be phenomenal for you and your business. This book shows you how to apply innovative tactics that you most likely aren't utilizing yet.

Chris and Eric Martinez are two of the hardest-working, most-honest men I've had the privilege to get to know throughout the years. As you're probably aware, there are too many people in our industry lacking character and integrity, but Chris and Eric are two world-class coaches who I'm honored to write this foreword for.

I'm also excited for YOU and YOUR journey. I know this book will not only take your online personal training business to new, modern heights, but it has the potential to change your life and the lives of every client you serve.

Mike Arce
CEO of Loud Rumor - The #1 Agency in Fitness
Host of The GSD Show

Preface

The Night Everything Changed

It's four in the morning, three days before Christmas, my identical twin and I are eighteen years old, seniors in high school, and everything in our lives is going so well; life couldn't be better. A priest and a police officer knock on our door, and we both run into our older brother's and parents' rooms to see if they're all there...Our father is not there.

My heart sinks to the floor, and I ask, "Where's my dad?"

The priest and the police officer sit the family down and tell us that our father has been killed in a car accident.

We can't process it, we can't breathe, is this a nightmare we are having, we are cold and have chills running down our spines, and our vision is blurry...the only thing we can hear is our mother screaming and crying, "Nooooooo!"

It was no nightmare we woke up from; our life has just been turned upside down as fast as you can snap your fingers.

We begin to realize that our eighteen years of happiness was just crushed, and for what reason? Nobody will ever know. That light of happiness just got a dark cloud over it, and we realized our family would never be the same again.

What hurt the most was never getting a chance to say goodbye to our father one last time.

We entered hell at the age of eighteen and knew we had a long road ahead of us to get back. We had the picture-perfect life, and now it was all gone and taken from us.

We knew that our ultimate provider, our leader, our role model to mold us into men, our father wasn't there to guide us in life anymore. We knew a piece of our mother went with him that night, and she would never be the same again. We knew our older brother would have to take on that father-figure role at such a young age and be robbed of anything else he planned on doing.

Three months after our father passed away, we found out our closest grandmother, our mom's mother, was diagnosed with cancer. Our grandmother battled her cancer for a few months and then passed away. Three years later, our grandma and grandpa on our dad's side passed away as well.

Another ton of bricks hit us, especially our mother; she was so lost and turned to alcoholism and antidepressants. It was one of the toughest things to see every day in our young lives, and it destroyed us for many years.

We could not understand why this was happening to our family.

Our Drive in Life

Growing up, we lived a very structured life with school, sports, church, and family time. Our father was a Correctional Officer at San Quentin State Prison before he passed away, so you can imagine he was pretty strict and made sure we had daily structure. He once told us, "Nothing in life will ever be given to you. You have to work for everything you want, and if it's too easy, then find something bigger that challenges you." Everything he had taught us up to that point would have to be practiced in the real world on our own. Trial and error, as society likes to call it.

Our father had a relentless mindset; he was the ultimate provider for our family and one hell of a role model to us. We watched our father's work ethic each and every day, and that rubbed off on us. When he passed away, we had our dark times; however, we found a way out because we were relentless as well. We knew we were always in the fight and would never quit. There are two choices you can make when adversity knocks on your door.

1. You get knocked down, play the victim role, and use that as a crutch to play small in life.
2. You get back up, keep going, and play up to your potential and play bigger in life.

We prevailed after many years of battling. It wasn't easy by any means. We still have our battles today and will continue to face many more.

After our father's death, we made a promise to ourselves that we would be there by our mother's side for however long it took us to graduate from the local Sonoma State University.

We would sacrifice going away to college, we would sacrifice getting the college experience by living on campus, we would sacrifice our dream to move to Southern California, and we would work to help pay tuition and bills at home.

This wasn't the way it was supposed to go down for us. But we survived the curveball, the tragedy that occurred, and we manned up and did what we had to do to get through it. We developed mental, emotional, and spiritual resilience that we never knew we had inside of us.

Rising up in Life and Leading Others

We wrote this book for several reasons. As you read along, it will all make sense. One reason is that over the past decade, fitness saved our lives through the tough times we went through. It not only physically made us stronger, but mentally. This also led us to become fitness coaches and build an empire of a fitness coaching business called "Dynamic Duo Training," where we have helped thousands of amazing clients around the world with their fitness goals over the last decade.

What's in It for You as a Fit Pro?

If you are willing to exchange the time it takes to serve others and really study this book, if you implement even a portion of the techniques we describe, we can guarantee you will add more Influence, Income, Impact, and Independence to your fitness coaching business.

We can make such bold promises because we have been in this game for a decade and have helped our Inner Circle students build successful coaching businesses with our tools and guidance.

What's in It for Us?

Our end goal is simple: trust and adding value. We would like to earn yours. And yes, we do have big dreams.

We would like to earn your trust by making you money first, if that's okay. We want to give you results in advance. Try just a couple of tactics from this book, watch them work, then try a few more, watch them work and so on. The more you see results in your own business, the better.

If this all sounds cool, let's continue into the book.

Introduction

The Best of Both Worlds as Fitness Professionals

We remember it as if it were yesterday when we opened our very own home gym in Orange County, California, in 2015. The excitement we had ordering the equipment, painting the garage, hiring the handyman to install mirrors and lights, and the smell of the rubber mats being laid down topped it off. We still get chills when we think about the possibilities that could have been with this home gym.

We had long-term plans to train a handful of clients while doing our online coaching a.k.a. The Hybrid Training Model.

We had plans to hire independent personal trainers, charge a monthly rent, and provide them with a state-of-the-art small training studio.

We had plans to hold health and fitness seminars for the local community.

And of course, we had plans to create tons of video content in the home gym.

During a celebration in Miami after renewing the year lease on the home in Orange County, we got a phone call before cracking open a bottle of champagne on beautiful South Beach, Miami. The landlord was calling to tell us he decided to sell the home and needed us out in thirty days.

Fast forward thirty days: we were out and so was the $10K gym.

Gone...

Poof! like dust...

We don't tell you this story to make you feel bad for us, but to inspire you about the possibilities within doing the Hybrid Training Model of in-person personal training and online training...the best of both worlds.

If you want to become a Dynamic Fit Pro, you have to start thinking about multiple income streams. The average millionaire has five to seven income streams.

Maybe getting to seven figures is your goal, maybe it isn't, but to become a six-figure earner in the fitness industry, the Hybrid Training Model is going to be your best way to get there.

You Can't Buy Experience

"There is no greater teacher than experience."- Lebron James

These days, the internet is like the Wild Wild West, literally. You have the good guys and the bad guys.

Some business coaches out there claim they can help you make six or seven figures in two to three months, some say they can get you hundreds of new paying high-ticket clients, and some even promise bigger…but you know what we tend to see happen a lot? A lot of over-promising and under-delivering and the brand being overhyped with subpar service.

Some of these business coaches have never even had a business themselves, invested money, lost money, coached clients online, or walked the walk. You, as a fitness professional, have to do your research on who you decide to invest in to take you and your business to the next level.

We have been in the fitness industry for a decade now. We started out as personal trainers from 2009–2011 at an independent gym in Rohnert Park, California called Warehouse Fitness. We then went on to co-found Dynamic Duo Training, an online fitness and health coaching business, in 2011. We have worked with over a thousand clients over the past decade and have had some of the cream of the crop fitness coaches as mentors (Dr. Layne Norton, Dr. Eric Helms, and Dr. Joe Klemczewski).

After serving and impacting thousands of lives of individuals within health and fitness, we had a huge passion to help develop fitness professionals into Dynamic Fit Pros. So, we invested hundreds of thousands of dollars in business masterminds such as the Tai Lopez Business Builder ($25,000 investment) and Cole Hatter's Connect Mastermind ($20,000), and then went on to hire business coaches in marketing, sales, social media, public speaking, personal branding, and more.

This has all led to where we are today: in the past three years, we have helped hundreds of fitness professionals take their business online and build a Hybrid Training Model to create more income, influence, impact, and independence within our Dynamic Inner Circle.

We have made $250,000 worth of mistakes, we have invested hundreds of thousands of dollars in coaches to accelerate the learning curve, we have impacted thousands of lives, and we are on a mission to create thousands of Dynamic Fit Pros.

The Why Behind Rise of the Fit Pros

We both have felt stuck on an island, lost, made excuses about not having any money, had self-doubt, and felt alone with zero guidance or direction with our vision as fitness coaches when we first got started. It's one of the worst feelings, and we can relate to you.

Headaches and frustration went along with trying to build our business all by ourselves and wear all the hats. We don't want you to make the same mistakes.

This is why we created The Dynamic Inner Circle to help Fit Pros like you build and grow a successful fitness coaching business. Our students in our Inner Circle program end up saving hundreds of thousands of dollars in mistakes while simultaneously shortening the learning curve to reach their desired level of success and play bigger in life as Fit Pros.

We are tired of seeing Fit Pros have scarcity mindsets, make excuses, have an ego, and be misled by other coaches when it comes to building their coaching businesses. We are sick and tired of seeing Fit Pros not rising to the occasion and playing bigger in all areas of life.

Our mission for this book is to share our gifts and expertise with you to help you build an empire of a fitness coaching business. We want you to have the same success we have achieved and know it is possible with our guidance, knowledge, and experience.

We want you to create More Income, Influence, Impact, and Independence. More importantly, free up more time, build expert status, create valuable, intentional, and shareable content on social media, and live a dynamic lifestyle.

All you have to do is Rise Up as a Fit Pro and play bigger in life and never quit when building your fitness coaching business.

We commend you for investing your time in this book, and we hope to gain your trust throughout it, and invite you to play bigger and be a part of the Rise of the Fit Pros community!

Are you ready to Rise Up as a Fit Pro and take what is yours?

Chapter 1
In-Person Personal Training

> *"Most people are looking for the elevator to success*
> *instead of taking the stairs."*
> —Zig Ziglar

When building a Hybrid Training Model, one of the common questions we get from our Inner Circle students is, "Should I do Online Training first or should I do In-Person Personal Training first?"

There's never going to be a black and white answer when starting your Hybrid Training Model. However, what we have seen work best is building your In-Person Personal Training business first, and here's why:

- You get to train people in person first before coaching people online. There's a difference between personal training someone face-to-face and one-to-one as opposed to coaching someone online.
- Some of the best online coaches personally train people one-on-one in person first, and they're able to carry that experience and skillset over to online coaching, which makes

them better coaches all around. Personal training in person for two years really helped us become some of the better online coaches out there.

- Communication with clients is vital for being a dynamic fit pro because clients buy coaches, not coaching. The chances of you enhancing your communication skills are much higher in person, which will only help you communicate better as an online coach.

The next question we get from our Inner Circle students is, "Now that I'm going to be doing personal training in person first, should I work at a commercial gym or independent gym?"

One of our main goals for our Inner Circle students is to help them become independent trainers at small boutique gyms.

Being an independent contractor instead of an employee allows for the following benefits:

- Scheduling freedom - working at a big box gym means you have set hours you need to be there. Being an independent trainer means setting your own schedule, days, times, and time off.
- Opportunity for other work - a flexible schedule allows for other opportunities, such as house calls, boot camps at parks, and training clients on the side.
- Personal and professional projects - at some point, you will start working on your online business, so you will need to find time blocks to be able to build this and other projects you are working on.
- Tax benefits - depending on where you live, you can write off business expenses, such as laptops, home office space,

workout clothes, and continuing education related to fitness, and possibly gym equipment.

- You get to create your own pricing models, packages, and billing cycles, which lead to higher pay than big-box gyms.

- You get to set your own billing cycles to find hidden profits and make payments psychologically easier for clients to pay, thus avoiding churn and keeping retention high.

- Facilities tend to be smaller, cleaner, and more well-appointed, which attracts higher-end, more dedicated clientele.

- More personalized management, which tends to attract career trainers who are serious about their work.

- You determine your income ceiling and potential through your creativity and ability to market and sell your services, as opposed to personal trainers at commercial gyms making an average of **$15–20 per hour** or **10–15%** of PT session rate.[1]

- Smaller, more intimate communities and tribes are built at boutique gyms as opposed to bigger box gyms, which leads to more trust and loyalty.

Now, this isn't to bash big box gyms. They serve a purpose for personal trainers as well, and many of our Inner Circle students started at big box gyms before transitioning to independent gyms. In fact if you have no experience as a personal trainer, we recommend at least one full year at a big box gym before going independent, for the following reasons:

---

[1] "WORLDWIDE SURVEY OF FITNESS TRENDS FOR 2019: ACSM's Health & Fitness Journal." *LWW*, journals.lww.com/acsm-healthfitness/Fulltext/2018/11000/WORLDWIDE_SURVEY_OF_FITN ESS_TRENDS_FOR_2019.6.aspx.

- You get to learn the ins and outs of the business.
- Clients are fed to you, so you don't have to worry about marketing and sales.
- Access to a lot of different clientele, which can help you determine what kind of niche you want to eventually serve.
- Access to a lot of equipment, so you don't have to invest in your own equipment right away.
- Educational opportunities and the ability to move up to more senior training positions.

A great real-life example of this is our Inner Circle student, Juan Salgado (@the_chosenjuan1). He started out as a PT at a big box gym, LA Fitness, in Orange County, California. He then transitioned to being an independent trainer at a smaller boutique-style gym, and he is now doing the Hybrid Training Model of coaching in person and online.

To sum up this chapter, there's never going to be a "perfect path" or "black and white answer" on which route to start on. We tend to follow what the data tells us. With working as independent trainers for and coaching hundreds of Fit Pros, it seems that starting as an in-person personal trainer first is the best step to take toward becoming a dynamic fit pro. Then you can go online and eventually strive to work as an independent trainer at a small boutique gym.

Fit Pro to Dynamic Fit Pro Tips

Start creating a spreadsheet of small boutique gyms around the city you want to eventually work at. Start building relationships with the owners, go train there, ask how you can help them in any way, figure out what unique ways you can help their gym, follow up with them, start building your resume, and when the time comes, your chances will be much higher to be an independent trainer there.

Please fill in the blank:

I'm going to Rise as a Fit Pro because

_____

Chapter 2
Starting Your Online Personal Training Business

"An effective leader spends his day working on his business and not in it."
—Bedros Keuilian

Accxording to the American College of Sports Medicine, online fitness and nutrition programs are gaining popularity and effectiveness, and the online fitness market is expected to grow from $849.60 million USD in 2017 to $2582.04 million USD by 2022.[2]

We can tell you that after working with over a thousand clients this past decade, both in person and online, online coaching is taking over due to being able to provide much more overall value. Rather than just showing clients how to execute workouts and count sets and reps as a personal trainer, with online coaching, you're looked at as a "fitness and health coach," which means you are dynamic! You can coach people on program design for training, you can give nutritional

---

[2] "WORLDWIDE SURVEY OF FITNESS TRENDS FOR 2019: ACSM's Health & Fitness Journal." *LWW*, journals.lww.com/acsm-healthfitness/Fulltext/2018/11000/WORLDWIDE_SURVEY_OF_FITN ESS_TRENDS_FOR_2019.6.aspx.

and supplementation advice, you can program cardiovascular protocols, you can give sleep and stress management advice…heck, even lifestyle tips here and there. Being an online coach allows you to be more dynamic as a Fit Pro.

With online coaching, the client receives both training and nutrition coaching, so long as the coach is qualified and has experience. With online coaching, the coach can create services and packages that include lifestyle coaching, sleep, or stress coaching. You can get as creative as you want.

Take Inner Circle student from London, Canada, Kyle Clarke (@theprimaltrainer). At the gym he was working for, all he could offer was private personal training. Now that he has his online business built out, he is offering training, nutrition, cardio protocols, and even private animal flow style and kettlebell training programs.

With online coaching, clients can reach a larger talent pool where they can find an online coach who is an expert and specializes in specific areas within fitness.

With online coaching, clients can follow their soon-to-be coach on social media these days to see if their coaching and personality will fit.

Now, this isn't to put online training on a pedestal and have you ditch your personal training job and be like, "I am going all-in on online, dude!"

It's not to say online training is easy and your ticket to "get rich quick."

Far from that…

That's why we are huge advocates of the Hybrid Training Model, which we will discuss in great detail in the next chapter.

The above data shows that online training has grown a tremendous amount and will continue to grow going forward, so we recommend you don't wait to get started with your online coaching business. Here are the three steps we teach our Inner Circle students that we recommend when building your online training business:

Step 1 - Learn the three-step online training framework

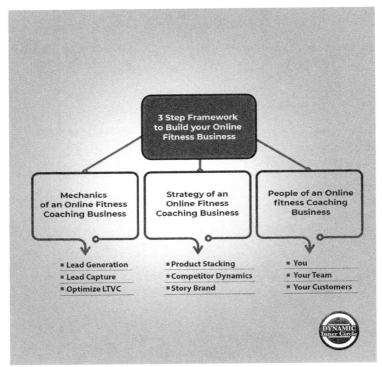

Mechanics of an Online Fitness Coaching Business
- You have to have a marketing plan to get online leads
- You have to have a sales process to be able to close the leads
- You have to deliver a massive customer experience to your online clients to retain them as Lifetime Valued Customers

Strategy of an Online Fitness Coaching Business
- Once you have your first choice of model of online training, which we will discuss in Step 2, and you have stabilized it, optimized it, and are ready to expand it, you can start

thinking of other products/services to stack and offer alongside it, but they need to be stacked properly in order to build a money-making machine

- With competitor dynamics, you or someone on your team needs to keep up with your competitors, do some market research, test ideas and concepts, and make sure you're constantly working on the business, not in the business, to scale.

- In the book *Start with Why*, Simon Sinek makes a great point that people buy WHY you do something not WHAT you do. In other words, people buy COACHES, not COACHING. So, you need to constantly work on your story brand because stories sell and facts tell. More on this in Chapter 4.

People in an Online Fitness Coaching Business

- It all starts with YOU, the owner and founder of the company. You have to have a strong CEO mindset and take care of yourself. We will dive deep into the importance of mindset in Chapter 9.

- People and personnel. With time, your business will grow and scale, and you will have to hire people or a team to help you, so you have to become a leader and be able to manage people and your team.

- Your customers are the lifeline of your business. If you don't serve and constantly give your clients value, an experience, and results, they won't pay, stay, or refer.

Step 2 - Identify what online coaching model you want to start with

- Individualized One-to-One Online Coaching
- Group Style Online Coaching
- High Ticket-Specific Promise, Result & Deadline

Now that you have a grasp on Step 1, let's dive into choosing which online coaching model you want to start with. Keep in mind to always start with just one of these coaching models and stabilize it, optimize it, and then think about expanding it. We made the mistake of trying to create too many products at once and spread ourselves thin (one of our many costly $250K mistakes).

- Individualized One-on-One Online Coaching - This is a direct carryover from private one-on-one personal training. However, coaching someone online is different than in-person training. In our opinion, after coaching thousands of clients online over the past eight years, this online coaching model is the best one to start with and allows you to generate income fast. An example of this model is an online coach who works individually with 5–40 clients online and charges $200–500 a month.

- Group Style Online Coaching - This is a direct carryover from semi-private personal training. There are a lot of ways to set up this one-to-many coaching model. You can coach 5–25 clients in a group fashion with a more hands-on approach, or you can come up with a lower price point offer to coach 25–100+ clients in a more automated, membership area, which is a less hands-on approach.

- High Ticket-Specific Promise, Results, and Deadline - This is a coaching model that will require you to deliver more value and more of your time, but will allow you to coach a smaller coaching cohort and charge a higher premium. We've found from our past experience, and with our Inner Circle students, that if you tie in a specific promise, a specific result, and a deadline, you can charge more for it because this becomes a transformation package. The specific promise and result are tied in with an emotional attachment and specific pain, and the deadline creates urgency within the program. An example of this model is an online coach who works individually with 5–10 clients online and charges $1,000+ depending on the specific promise, result, and deadline.

Our Inner Circle student, Jeff Toledo (@toledo_fit) from New Jersey, chose to do a group style online coaching model where he's incorporating his special method HIET (High Intensity Explosive Training) and offering this to a group of ten or more online clients.

Step 3 - Implement the 10-step online training business basic processes

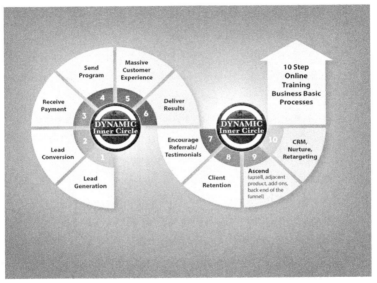

Now that you have a grasp on Step 2, let's dive into putting this all into a legit online training system and process:

1. Lead Generation - You have to have a marketing plan to get online leads, whether that's through Facebook, Instagram, YouTube, LinkedIn, Pinterest, Snapchat, Google, blogs, podcasts, referrals, etc.

2. Lead Conversion - You have to have a sales process to be able to close the leads that you are generating with either phone

calls, email campaigns, Skype/Zoom calls, landing pages, etc.

3. Receive Payment - Set up an online merchant account such as PayPal, Stripe, or Venmo to receive payments from clients and make sure to have a proper billing cycle in place.

4. Send Programs - You can send programs through online training software such as Trainerize, True Coach, or Coach Catalyst, or you can send programs through Google, upload PDFs, Word Docs or Excel sheets to DropBox or Microsoft One Drive.

5. Massive customer experience - You must deliver an emotional and Ritz-Carlton-like experience to your clients just as you would in person. Send them small gifts throughout their journey with you, use video and audio to communicate, jump on the phone, FaceTime, or Zoom calls with them. Learn more in-depth tactics on customer experience in Chapter 7.

6. Deliver results - Just as you would get your client(s) results with in-person training, you must get them results online too. If they don't get results, they won't pay, stay, or refer.

7. Encourage referrals and testimonials - Referrals online are a huge part of your marketing strategy because they keep marketing spend down, and a referral is considered a very hot lead in which your chances to close are much higher. So, don't be afraid to ask for referrals from your online clients. Ask for video testimonials of their fitness journey and work with you. Don't forget to ask permission to share their before and after pics on social media and on your site.

8. Retention - Everyone likes to brag about getting new clients, but you know what people don't like to mention? Their retention rate. Our retention rate has helped us sustain a six-

figure coaching business for nearly a decade. If you give your clients a massive customer experience, deliver results, and build a genuine and caring relationship with them, they will continue to pay, stay, and refer.

9. Ascend - Once you have stabilized and optimized your one core online model and are ready to expand, you can start to think about adjacent products, such as a course, do-it-yourself program, ebook, membership service, etc. Now you can start creating more income streams within your online business. More on this in Chapter 6.

10. CRM, Nurture, Retargeting - Now that you have all nine systems and processes built within your online training business, it's vital that you create a Customer Relationship Management (CRM) system to keep track of potential leads, current clients, and past clients. We recommend starting this by using a spreadsheet and then getting fancier with time and using CRM tools, such as Infusionsoft, Pipedrive, or Hub Spot. Once you have your spreadsheet of leads, current clients, and past clients, you must nurture these leads by checking in with them, following up, and sending them value. If you are running paid ads (FB, IG, YT or Google), it's very important to create a retargeting campaign to warm your prospects up to eventually buy from you.

Other Online Training Models:

Hybrid Training (learn more in Chapter 3)

- Hybrid Training allows you to open up two income streams to generate more income.

- It allows you to not put all your eggs in one basket, such as going all-in on online training, so you can easily transition to online training from in-person personal training.
- It gives you the ability to create more time and freedom in your schedule.
- It gives clients a more affordable option besides private training.

Group Transformation Programs (GTP)
- These are great if you really want to niche down with a specific population and promote a specific goal with a specific deadline. Example: "Lose 10 pounds in 6 weeks and get fit for Summer Vacation!"
- GTP doesn't require much of your time or hands-on since it's a group-style coaching and not so individualized.
- GTP is more affordable for clients to join.
- Some clients love the group comradery and community feel with large coaching groups.
- With the right systems and marketing strategy, this model can be automated and scaled.

One-Off Programs
- An example of a one-off program is if someone didn't want to do your individualized or group coaching and just wanted you to program them a training and/or nutrition program to follow.
- These are nice downsells if people can't afford your higher ticket offers.
- These are nice continuation programs to offer once clients are done with your higher ticket programs.

On-Demand Workouts (ODW)

- Think Peleton and Les Mills livestream workouts. You can watch your clients work out live via Skype or Zoom video.
- ODW is great if you run larger group style workouts, such as boot camp–style, HIIT workouts, yoga, or circuit-style training.
- ODW is awesome if you enjoy working out side-by-side (technically) with your clients, correcting their form, and motivating them.
- ODW could have some issues as far as client/instructor video meet-up times and issues with filming at a gym.

A perfect example is Inner Circle student Mark Nendick from Canada (@mark_nendick). He thought outside of the box and took action by creating an online corporate health program where he's making a lot of impact and income.

We hope you take the above three steps into action as this framework is a proven system that has helped us grow and sustain Dynamic Duo Training over the past eight years. We have helped hundreds of Fit Pros like you within our Inner Circle build a legitimate Online Training Business.

Fit Pro to Dynamic Fit Pro Tips

When you start building your online coaching business, have the mindset of building a business for the long haul—three years, five years, even a decade or more. There is no overnight sensation in this business. It takes time, hard work like building your physique, building a solid reputation, treating people right, being ethical, constantly learning and growing, and a relentless mindset to never throw in the towel.

Please fill in the blank:

I'm going to Rise as a Fit Pro because

_____

Chapter 3
Setting Up Your Hybrid Training Model in Four Steps

"Make a 10X effort in everything you do. Outwork people.
10X levels of massive action."
—Grant Cardone

According to a *2019* review from the *ACSM Worldwide Survey of Fitness Trends*, personal trainers make an average of $15–20 per hour or 10–15% of a personal training session. We're almost 100% confident that this was for PTs who worked for commercial or big box gyms.[3]

Another PT salary finding on *Balancareers.com* shows that the average personal trainer makes $47,700, which is slightly above the median salary in the U.S. in 2019.[4]

---

[3] "WORLDWIDE SURVEY OF FITNESS TRENDS FOR 2019: ACSM's Health & Fitness Journal." *LWW*, journals.lww.com/acsm-healthfitness/Fulltext/2018/11000/WORLDWIDE_SURVEY_OF_FITN ESS_TRENDS_FOR_2019.6.aspx.
[4] Doyle, Alison. "How Much Is the Average Salary for US Workers?" *The Balance Careers*, The Balance Careers, 10 May 2019,

Moreover, our friend and CEO, Jonathan Goodman *(if you're interested in hearing our interview with him, see this link https://tinyurl.com/ygnvxk9z)* of the Personal Training Development Center did a survey with over 1,000 personal trainers that shows that the average PT session was between $50–70 US per hour. They also revealed that those who trained at small boutique gyms made more money than personal trainers at big box gyms. They also showed that when you do Hybrid Training, you make more overall income per year.[5]

If we go back to some of the online training predictions from ACSM, online fitness and nutrition programs are gaining popularity and effectiveness, and the online fitness market is expected to grow from $849.60 million USD in 2017 to $2,582.04 million USD by 2022. They also reported that the median pay for an online trainer is $39,210 annually.

Let's do some math here. We know, math wasn't our strongest subject either…

Say you combine the average PT annual salary $48K + part-time online trainer $20K = $68K

Or say a full-time online trainer annual salary $39K + part-time personal trainer $24K = $63K

---

www.thebalancecareers.com/average-salary-information-for-us-workers-2060808.

[5] Schuler, Lou. "Which Personal Trainers Earn the Most? We Have the Answer." *The PTDC*, 2 Sept. 2019, www.theptdc.com/personal-trainer-salary-survey.

You end up making more overall income per year. It's an additional $15–20K per year! An additional $15–20K per year can be life-changing and create more independence, travel, and time with family and loved ones.

Enter the Hybrid Training Model!

If this term is new to you, get used to it because soon you will be hearing it more often, especially from us because this is the model we saw working for us when we first started out way back in 2009. This is the model that is now working for our Dynamic Inner Circle students and their fitness coaching businesses.

(Here's a pic of our beautiful home gym we built and did the hybrid model with in Orange County - See video here: https://youtu.be/Qm4xxoNX2YQ)

We have many of our personal trainer students making great money, building some awesome businesses with a Hybrid Training Model, and impacting more lives than ever—they are happy campers.

Here are all the pros of building a hybrid model of in-person personal training and online personal training:
- You automatically have two revenue streams (Mo Money, Mo Money!)

- You can work remotely with your online clients.
- You can work in person with your clients and have that face-to-face communication, which is awesome.
- You can set your own prices, packages, and billing cycles within each coaching business.
- You can stack your offers and use value ladders to charge a premium for both in-person and online.
- You can set your own hours with in-person clients now that time is freed up with remote clients.
- You can take on as many clients as you want remotely to make a greater impact.
- You can do group training both in person and online.
- You control your own programming (training and nutrition).
- You can port your in-person clients over to your online coaching later down the road.
- You will get more referrals from both coaching businesses.
- You will develop an in-person and online community of people.
- You stay sharp on both skill sets as a personal trainer (online and in-person).
- You can later build more automated-digital and scalable fitness products since you have a base of hot buyers now from both in-person and online training.
- You have the best of both worlds, so you can help and impact more lives altogether.

Just to be fair, we will list out the cons of a Hybrid Training Model:
- You can be limited by location as you meet with clients in person regularly or depending on the structure of your hybrid model.

- Sometimes a tough sell to certain clients who don't understand or aren't open to trying online training with in-person training.
- Hybrid Training works better as an independent trainer.

By creating a hybrid model of in-person personal training and online personal training you seriously have the best of both worlds as a personal trainer.

Now, you might think, Is this too good to be true, twins? What's the catch?

We are honest guys and terrible liars, so we must be honest here, there is one drawback, but it's very minor.

The best way for this Hybrid Training Model to work in your favor is if you train clients in person as an "independent personal trainer."

Why as an independent trainer? (see Chapter 1 again for the benefits of independent training)

- You are not an employee for a corporate/commercial gym.
- You don't get robbed of what you make revenue-wise.
- You set your own prices, memberships, packages, billing cycle, etc.
- You pay monthly rent and keep the rest of your profits.
- You have to hustle to get your own clients, thus you learn sales and marketing skills.
- You set your own schedule.
- You build a community of your own.
- Clients feel more comfortable in smaller gyms.
- You can control the outcomes of your clients once they are done with your services.
- You don't have a boss or head trainer trying to steal the spotlight.

Now, don't get discouraged if you are not an independent personal trainer yet. Many of our Inner Circle students are training their clients from an LA Fitness, Equinox, 24 Hour Fitness, Gold's Gym, Crunch, etc. and still building a hybrid model of in-person personal training and online personal training businesses until they find another gig as an independent personal trainer.

So, if you are in the same boat, it is totally fine, you can still start building out this powerful hybrid model and play the long game with it. Don't use this as an excuse.

"But Chris and Eric, I don't know how or where to start with building a hybrid model!"

Don't worry, we got you…

Step 1: Identify what Hybrid Training Model you want to do.

- > Remote Hybrid
- > 80/20 Hybrid
- > Best of Both Worlds Hybrid
- > Extra Cash Hybrid

- Remote Hybrid - Think of this as being a full-time online trainer and doing some in-person personal training. An example of this would be a full one-on-one online training client load of 20–30 clients and a small in-person load of 3–5 clients per week.

- 80/20 Hybrid - In an 80/20 Hybrid Training Model, your clients only come in 20% of the time—X amount of times per week/bi-monthly/monthly—to train with you (*all depends on how many times you want them to come in*) and have you do in-person assessments, teach new exercises, review and correct form, and answer training and nutrition questions. The other 80% is online training (weekly check-ins, training/nutrition programming, support group, constant communication via phone/email/video, etc.).

- Best of Both Worlds Hybrid - This is the sweet spot in our opinion. We have seen this work over and over with our Inner Circle students. You are taking on a similar client load of in-person and online clients. For example, you train 10–20 people in person and 10–20 people online.

- Extra Cash Hybrid - Think of this as being a full-time in-person personal trainer and doing some online training. An example of this would be a full one-on-one private training client load of approximately 20 clients and a small online training client load of approximately 5 clients.

Step 2: Figure out where you want to do your in-person personal training.

- Big Box Gym (24 Hour Fitness, LA Fitness, Golds, Equinox, Crunch)
- Boutique gyms (small studios, clean, well equipped, good locations)
- In-home training (go to people's homes and train them)
- Neighborhood community centers (places like luxury apartment gyms, park districts or community fitness centers)

- Corporate Wellness (find corporations that are looking for team or group training once or twice per week)

Step 3: Identify your Online Training Model

- ● Individualized One-to-One Online Coaching
- ● Group Style Online Coaching
- ● High Ticket-Specific Promise, Result & Deadline

- Individualized One-on-One Online Coaching - This is a direct carryover from private one-on-one personal training. However, coaching someone online is different than in-person training. In our opinion, after coaching thousands of clients online over the past eight years, this online coaching model is the best one to start with and allows you to generate income fast. An example of this model is an online coach who works individually with 5–40 clients online and charges $200–500 a month.

- Group Style Online Coaching - This is a direct carryover from semi-private personal training. There are a lot of ways to set up this one-to-many coaching model. You can coach 5–25 clients in a group fashion with a more hands-on approach, or you can come up with a lower price point offer to coach 25–100+ clients in a more automated, membership area, which is a less hands-on approach.

- High Ticket-Specific Promise, Results, and Deadline - This is a coaching model that will require you to deliver more value and more of your time, but will allow you to coach a smaller coaching cohort and charge a higher premium. We've found from our past experience, and with our Inner Circle students, that if you tie in a specific promise, a specific result, and a deadline, you can charge more for it because this becomes a transformation package. The specific promise and result are tied in with an emotional attachment and specific pain, and the deadline creates urgency within the program. An example of this model is an online coach who works individually with 5–10 clients online and charges $1,000+ depending on the specific promise, result, and deadline.

Step 4: Get Started Today by Doing the Following:

- Start by getting very clear as to who you want to work with, your ideal client (see Chapter 5)
- Figure out your Unique Selling Proposition (USP) as a personal trainer (what makes your skill set different and what specific problems do you solve?)
- Create Badass content that is Valuable, Intentional, and Shareable so you can get social media followers to Know, Like, And Trust you and hire you (see Chapter 8)
- Start creating a buzz to your social media following, current clients, newsletters, and community that you are using a Hybrid Training Model, this way they can have a choice as to how they want to work with you (see Chapter 8)
- Start porting over your in-person clients to your online coaching business if they no longer need you for in-person, are planning to travel, or need to downgrade from personal training
- Ask your in-person clients for referrals to build your online platform
- Get good at omnichannel strategies, meaning start reaching out to leads, referrals, and prospects through various channels (social media, email, text software, local events, chatbots, etc.)

Inner Circle student Colten Tyler from Scottsdale, CA (@colten.fitcoach) started very strategically when building his Hybrid Training Model. He used some of his in-person training clients and put them in an 8-week online training test group, got them results, tested his methods, received social proof, and now he can build his online training program off this.

We could go on with the list above as to how to get started building a Hybrid Training Model, but we are pretty sure we got your wheels spinning with these four steps. The hard truth is, none of it matters if you don't take action!

Fit Pro to Dynamic Fit Pro Tips

When you have both your in-person and online training businesses set up, make sure to create a private Facebook group so you can create a massive community. This is one of the beauties of the Hybrid Training Model. With two communities, people can share the ups and downs, network, and even become lifelong friends.

Please fill in the blank:

I'm going to Rise as a Fit Pro because

_____

Chapter 4
Storytelling, Your Why, and a Vision

"Most people get stuck in an almost state, an almost life.
Don't be like most people."
—Ray Dalio

Facts Tell, Stories Sell

When we first heard this from our mentor Mark Lack, it took us a few moments to really grasp what that meant, but once it clicked, it made total sense. To this day, we stand by that statement and we suggest you take a mental pic of it.

When you stop and think of the best marketing and advertising companies, such as Apple, Coca-Cola, McDonald's, and Amazon.com, they all do a great job of telling stories, which leads to emotions, relatability, and trust for the consumer. Once the trust is established, it's game over and they become buyers and sometimes lifetime buyers. You may not even realize it, but it's all done through the power of storytelling, not telling facts and selling a bunch of benefits.

We remember how much we used to struggle with this, but once we started sharing our story about how we lost our father, battled adversity, and how fitness saved our lives, so many people appreciated us being vulnerable. This broke down barriers and led to trust. We learned to turn our messes into our messages.

This is the same thing we drill home to all of our Inner Circle students who are trying to become better fitness marketers. We all have a story to tell and share with the world. Each and every one of you awesome fitness professionals has a story to share with your past clients, current clients, and future clients. Here is what you can use to get your wheels spinning:

- Why did I get into fitness?
- What led me to be a fitness coach?
- What kind of pain was I going through, and how did fitness help me get out of that pain?
- How do I now help my clients get out of that similar pain?

These are all great questions to think about. They can help you get started sharing and telling more stories within your brand, marketing, and advertising as a Fit Pro!

An exercise we have all of our Inner Circle students do is audio record their stories. At first, it could be a bit uncomfortable, but that is what ultimately leads to growth, so get used to being uncomfortable. You can literally do this on your phone, computer, or tablet. Just tell your story and use the questions above to help guide you. Once you are done, have the audio transcribed through Rev.com so you can read it over and over to get familiar with it. This leads to creating content around your story and sharing it.

Once you have mastered your own story around your fitness brand, start creating more stories around your particular programs, offers, your daily struggles, share your client testimonials and their stories…the list goes on.

The cool thing about today is you have so much access to different social media platforms to share your story on especially if you are doubling down on video! It's a game-changer and will instantly separate you from other Fit Pros who are camera shy. Nothing against those who are camera shy; it's a skill you have to perfect and just takes reps and sets.

If there is one thing you take from sharing your story, it's Facts tell, Stories sell! It's that simple, so please start sharing your story more, connecting, and impacting more lives out there.

Student Story:
We want to share an example of our awesome Inner Circle student Hieu Phan's story. Hieu (@emergentfitrx) is a personal and online trainer along with being a pharmacist. His coaching business is Emergent Fitness. He has such an amazing story we helped him unlock.

Hieu came from Vietnam to Atlanta, Georgia at a young age to seek a better life in the States. Hieu grew up with a relentless work ethic of helping his family with bills, working full-time, and studying to become a pharmacist. He battled some adversity along the way and pushed through it.

Hieu recently took a huge step forward and moved to Southern California to seek his dreams and goals while leaving his family behind. Hieu is now doing extremely well with his fitness coaching business and living his dream here in sunny So Cal.

We could go more in-depth on his story, but we want you to see why telling and sharing your story with others is so powerful and how it can impact and inspire so many people.

Think about how many people can relate to Hieu's story and say to themselves, "Wow, if he could do that, so can I!"

Start With Why

Now that you have bought into the power behind storytelling and how you are a badass at sharing yours, it's time to really stop and think about what your BIG WHY is behind your brand. If you have not read the book *Start With Why* by Simon Sinek, please read it; it's a game-changer.

People don't buy what you do, they buy why you do it. Another way we like to put it is people buy coaches, not coaching. You, as a Fit Pro, are giving your clients hope, guidance, accountability, your expertise, and ultimately, confidence.

As a business, you must know WHY, HOW, and WHAT. This all starts with WHY you are doing this and WHY you are a Fit Pro. Here are some questions we recommend you take some time to answer:

- What is your purpose, cause, or belief?
- Why do your business and brand exist, and why should people care?
- Why do you get out of bed every morning to help others, and why should anyone care?

A *WHY* is just a belief.

HOWs are the actions you take to realize that belief.

WHATs are the results of those actions (products, services, marketing, culture).

Once you have answered these questions, it will bring a lot more clarity to what your true WHY is. This is very powerful because when times get tough in your business, you always have your why to fall back on. If it truly is that powerful, you will overcome any obstacle thrown your way because you are relentless about the movement you are creating and you believe in your WHY so much that nothing else matters.

One of our awesome Inner Circle students, Angela Devon (@angdevon), first came to us wanting to be a Fit Pro and help change people's lives through yoga, health, and fitness, but she was unclear as to why she wanted to help others. There are many Fit Pros in Angela's situation, so it's ok to be unclear at first.

What we did with Angela was take her through our "8-Step Framework" Process. We had her do a brain dump of all the reasons why she loved fitness, helping others, her story, how it's helped her, and what kind of legacy she wants to leave. After we brought her WHY to life, everything made more sense for her brand, business, and messaging when it came to her marketing and advertising, and now she is doing amazing things as a Fit Pro!

A huge mistake we used to make was not speaking our WHY from our hearts. We just spoke about it very generically. There's a big difference when you speak about your why from the inside out, rather than the outside in. You have to believe in your product and coaching abilities or nobody else will. Make sure to speak that shit from your heart because people can tell the difference.

Great leaders know how to win people's hearts instead of their minds and inspire others. Be the Fit Pro that inspires your clients and is playing bigger in life to create this amazing movement and culture that people want to be a part of and rave about.

Creating a Badass Vision

Now you are clear on what your story is and how to tell it. Now you know what your WHY is. It's so powerful that nothing can get in the way of your pursuits and stop you. Awesome! We are loving how you are rising as a Fit Pro, so let's keep going.

A vision is about creating a short statement or painting a picture that will guide you over the next three to five years, or even longer. It should be specific enough to say something about what you will do and equally what you will not do. Your vision should be capable of driving you to achieve a goal and be motivational so that you have a constant reminder of what you are trying to achieve when the going gets tough.

Without a vision, a goal is like a ship without a rudder, in danger of drifting aimlessly and potentially sinking. Joel A. Baker said, "Vision without action is merely a dream. Action without vision just passes the time. Vision with action can change the world." Many people lack a clear vision, and so they tend to jump from task to task without a clear understanding of what bonds the individual actions together and/or the value created by the individual actions. Your vision should provide the cornerstone for everything that you do and your goals in life.

Through the years, we have learned that if you think about strategy (the "how") too early, it will actually inhibit your vision (the "what") and block you from thinking as big as you need to think. What you need is a vision that is so BIG, it scares you, that is compelling, not only to others but to you as well. If it's not compelling, you won't have the motivation to stay the course, and you won't be able to recruit others to help you.

If you truly are a leader as a Fit Pro, understand that all leaders have two things:

1. A vision of the world that does not exist
2. The ability to communicate their vision to the world

Something we have our Inner Circle students do when it comes to getting clear on their vision is called Reverse Engineering a Vision. We invite you to try this as well on a piece of paper or a whiteboard. Have fun with it and think big!

- **Start with your five-year vision** (What are your goals around your business? How much do you want to make? What's something personal you want to accomplish? What's something fun?)
- **Next is your three-year vision** (What are your goals around your business? How much do you want to make? What's something personal you want to accomplish? What's something fun?)
- **Next is your one-year vision** (What are your goals around your business? How much do you want to make? What's something personal you want to accomplish? What's something fun?)

- **Next is your six-month vision** (What are your goals around your business? How much do you want to make? What's something personal you want to accomplish? What's something fun?)

- **Finally, your three-month vision** (What are your goals around your business? How much do you want to make? What's something personal you want to accomplish? What's something fun?)

Now that you are clear with all of these, you Reverse Engineer them and start with your five, three, and one-year goals, then your six-month goal, and finally, your three-month goal. Start chipping away and enjoy the journey leading to your vision.

If you really want to be great at anything, you have to have a clear vision of exactly what you want, why you want it, and when you want it to happen. All of our amazing mentors have done this and created a clear vision.

Think about how many athletes grow up idolizing legendary professionals; we know we did. How many of us wanted to be the next Michael Jordan, Serena Williams, Ronda Rousey, Peyton Manning, or Kobe Bryant? We are sure many people in the world envisioned themselves being like these hall-of-famer athletes, but realize at some point in their lives they cannot be. You can absolutely be great like them with hard work and talent, but chances are you will never be who they are, what they accomplished, and have their mindset and visions. You have to create your own vision as a Fit Pro. We are all meant to write a different story and live a life worth telling a story about.

Don't ever sell yourself short on your vision! Anything is possible with hard work, having amazing people around you, and being relentless about your goals and dreams in life.

Fit Pro to Dynamic Fit Pro Tips

Master your own story and storytelling around your fitness brand. Audio record your story and get it transcribed for content creation. Do a brain dump and get very clear on what your WHY is behind your brand and as a Fit Pro. Then learn to speak it from the inside out, not the outside in. Reverse engineer your vision, think big, get clear, then work your way up to each one.

Please fill in the blank:

I'm going to Rise as a Fit Pro because

_____

Chapter 5
Identifying Your Avatar and Specialty as a Fit Pro

"Understand and learn the basics and fundamentals first before getting into advanced concepts."
—Naval Ravakant

Who Is Your Customer?

How many times have you heard people say, "You have to niche down on your avatar to stand out"? If you haven't already, we're here to give you this advice. When we first heard this, we didn't put two and two together and execute it. It was probably our ego, we kid you not. Although we were still able to acquire over one hundred online clients combined, it was very confusing working with all sorts of clients instead of just niching down and serving one avatar. Lesson learned going forward. This chapter will save you from the mistakes we made.

Let's first dive into how to identify your customer. In our Dynamic Inner Circle Program, this is something we can really go deep on with our Fit Pros as part of our 8-Step Framework, and it creates a ton of clarity going forward.

When you are trying to identify your ideal avatar, a.k.a. customer, first take into consideration who you really enjoy working with and who you can best serve; stay in your lane as a coach.

In Chapters 1–3, we went deep on In-Person PT, Online PT, and our favorite, the Hybrid Training Model of both in-person and online training. Whichever one you choose to do, take these examples into consideration when looking to identify your avatar:

- Sports Performance
- General Health and Lifestyle
- Body Recomposition
- Physique Competitors
- Corrective Pain Management
- Fat Loss

These are core markets where your customers can be found. We recommend choosing no more than two of these, otherwise, it starts to get very difficult when creating your specialty as a Fit Pro, identifying your customers' pain points, and speaking directly to them through your messaging.

Once you have figured out your core markets, take a step further and ask yourself these questions:

- What age ranges are my customers?
- Are they only male or female?
- Do they have a specific career or are they a stay at home mom/dad?
- Where do they hang out?
- What are their hobbies?

- Do they have money and time to invest in a fitness coach?
- Are they serious about making a change?

What Are My Customer's Specific Problems?

Now that you have more clarity on who your customer is, this is where the fun part comes in: identifying their specific problems and pain points for you to solve.

The reason why you need to figure out what your customer's pain points are is to really speak their language through your messaging and content. It has to be so crystal clear to where they literally say, "Wow! I felt like so-and-so was speaking right to me."

A big mistake we see Fit Pros doing is speaking to a wider audience of people rather than identifying who their customer is, their specific pain points, and how they can get them out of that pain.

To really stand out today as a Fit Pro, you have to be very intentional and specific with your messaging and who you're speaking to. Don't be the Fit Pro trying to cater to everyone's needs. Be a specialist at what you do and who you talk to. This will help you stand out. All you need is 1,000 true fans who are loyal to you; you don't need the entire world.

An exercise we recommend you do is a brain dump on your avatar's specific problems and pain points once you have more clarity from answering the questions above. You will be surprised by how many pain points you can come up with and how you can solve them. The best part is you have great content right in front of you to use all over social media. Pick one pain point, talk about, tell a story, and talk about how you can solve it. You will see customers starting to ask you for more details about your coaching services because you spoke to them without you even knowing.

What's Your Specialty as a Fit Pro?

This is another mistake we see Fit Pros making today, so please pay attention here and get serious about what your specialty is. We like to use the following analogy with people when it comes to specialists. Who do you think earns a larger salary, a heart surgeon or general MD? The heart surgeon does because it's a very specific problem they are solving and a very specific pain they need to get the patient out of. This is how you have to start thinking like a dynamic fit pro.

We are big on Brain Dumps, so start writing down all the different things you are great at as a Fit Pro and what your specialty could be to help your ideal customers with. Some examples could be:

- Kettlebell training only
- HIIT Workouts only
- Bodyweight workouts only
- Glute training only
- Intermittent fasting only
- Macros only
- Keto Diets only

Do you see where we are going with this? Literally, come up with your specialty as a Fit Pro and how do you get people out of pain. What's your process like? What's the big promise for your clients? Dig deep on this! This is what will make you stand out and easily attract the right customers for you to serve.

Inner Circle Student Example

Let's use an example of one of our Inner Circle students, Adrian Ceja (@adrianceja_). Adrian is running a Hybrid PT Model in Anaheim, CA. When Adrian joined our program, he was very unclear as to who he truly wanted to work with and what his specialty was. After we took Adrian through an intensive coaching day and our 8-Step Framework, everything made sense. He knew who he wanted to work with and why. Here's what we came up with for Adrian's ideal avatar, their pain points, and his specialty:

- General Health, Lifestyle, and Fat Loss as his core market
- High Achiever Business Men ages 30–50 years old
- Pain points: Lack of confidence, no time, no energy, don't feel sexy, have no accountability, want to have a six-pack
- Adrian's specialty: Strength Training and Core Focus and Keto Diets

Now, stop and think about how much more clear this is and how he can now speak intentionally when he goes to market himself as opposed to speaking to everyone!

Adrian can now literally write up content all around the specific pain points he has addressed with his avatar and can talk directly to them about how he can get them out of their pain, guide them, and paint the picture with his specialty and more.

It's truly a thing of beauty when you get clear on who you want to work with, their pain points, and how you can help them with your specialty. That's how you stand out as a Fit Pro today!

How to Reach Celebrity Status Within Your Niche

Now that you have your niche and specialty nailed down, we really advocate for you to think about positioning. How do you want your ideal niche and customers to perceive you?

Here's an infographic we teach in our VIP day sessions:

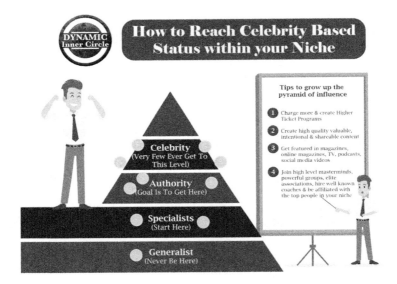

As you can see at the bottom of the pyramid, being perceived as a "Generalist" is a big no-no as a dynamic fit pro. If you made it this far, you are more clear on your niche and specialty. An example of a generalist is pretty much every personal trainer or online coach who will take on any client and say, "I help you lose fat and build muscle." So dull and generic, right? So never, ever, be a generalist; your niche will perceive you like every other PT and online PT out there.

Moving up the pyramid, you have being a "Specialist." That's what we just taught you in this chapter, so you can be perceived as more valuable than a regular and general Fit Pro. However, is this level truly going to get you positioned as that go-to-person in your niche?

Moving on up, now we start getting into the money-making levels, being perceived as an "Authority" and "Celebrity" in your niche and within your specialty. This is where your customers will pay top dollar to have you coach them online or train them in person because, in their eyes, you are the authority, the expert, the "go-to" person. This allows you to position yourself with celebrity status.

Think about some Fit Pros who have really done a great job of positioning themselves as the celebrity go-to experts within their niche and specialty:

- Layne Norton was the go-to guy for contest prep, getting competitors ripped to step on stage because he wrote for *Muscular Development* magazine, was featured on Bodybuilding.com, and worked with some pretty big-influential competitors.
- Jillian Michaels positioned herself as a celebrity trainer because, not only did she work with Hollywood celebrities, but all of the books she wrote, TV appearances, and DVDs she created allowed her to position herself as the expert trainer in fat loss with her specialty style of exercising,
- Shawn T of *Insanity* is looked at as an "authority and celebrity" Fit Pro because he sold millions of copies of his hit *Insanity* workout. This workout led people to perceive Shawn had a specialty within his exercise methodology, and they tied that in with him being on video and having his

own DVD. He positioned himself as an expert within that specific niche.

I think you get the point by now on why positioning yourself as an Authority or Celebrity within your niche and specialty can lead you to become a dynamic fit pro.

Use the tips from this chapter to help you work on positioning yourself and working up the pyramid of influence.

Fit Pro to Dynamic Fit Pro Tips

Get very clear on who your customer is by answering the questions in this chapter. Do a brain dump on all the specific pain points and problems your customer has. Identify what your specialty as a Fit Pro is so you can stand out. Work on getting to the authority and celebrity status levels of influence.

Please fill in the blank:

I'm going to Rise as a Fit Pro because

_____

Chapter 6
Money-Making Opportunities and Online Pricing and Packaging

"It is your responsibility at the helm of a business to squeeze maximum profits from it. That's your job."
—Dan Kennedy

In the last five chapters, our goal was to have you understand the concepts within them before we introduce you to all the money-making opportunities within the Hybrid Training Model. Now you understand what online training model you are going to choose and build upon. Now you have your hybrid training model identified. And now that you have your big why and vision, along with your specific niche and specialty within it...Let's make some money, shall we?

Digital Products

Online courses are great for getting people into your funnel who aren't ready to do your Hybrid Training coaching. We recommend four- to eight-week courses. Get very creative with them around your brand, specialty, and methods. You can build these off ClickFunnels, My Kajabi, Teachable, or Thinkific. After the course is over, you can upsell customers into your Hybrid Training coaching.

Do-It-Yourself Programs are cool because they are a nice way to push clients over the edge during sales consultations as a bonus. These are good continuation programs for clients who can't stay in your Hybrid Training Model. These can be built off training software like Trainerize, True Coach, or Excel Sheets and PDFs. We recommend 8–12 week do-it-yourself programs for training, nutrition, and cardio. You can get very creative with them around your brand, specialty, and methods.

Continuity Models are great for keeping clients. We are in the Netflix, Disney Plus, and Apple TV+ age, so why not join the trends and create your own fitness continuity program? *Hence, we created our version of the Netflix of Fitness Business (DynamicInnerCircle.com/Mentorship).* These can be password protected and exclusive membership sites, such as ClickFunnels, My Kajabi, Thinkific, or Light Speed VT. You can get as creative as you want with the offers and what they get monthly within their subscriptions. These are great for continuation programs and low barrier entry points to get people into your funnel and push them over the edge as a bonus.

Supplements are something many clients value. As sad as this is, a lot of your future clients have a higher perceived emotional attachment to supplements than to coaching, so you might as well sell supplements to them. You don't have to sell them BS supplements that have zero validity in the scientific literature, but the very few that are tried and true, why not? Companies like Dotfit.com, network marketing companies (Isagenix, Herbalife), local supplement stores, and online supplement companies have affiliate programs. Trust us, after working with over a thousand clients over the past decade, we shot ourselves in the foot for not selling supplements and creating another income stream out of it.

Physical Products

You can go the route of eCommerce (Shopify or Amazon) and sell physical products, such as shaker bottles, gym swag, apparel, etc. You can get affiliate links from exercise equipment companies, plug them into your YouTube videos and social media, and make some extra income. At the gym you train at, you can sell your own apparel, shaker bottles, towels, etc.

You can put on local or virtual workshops, events, and clinics, and teach on training/nutrition, take them through a training session, etc. Charge a low entry fee and sell on the back end into your Hybrid Training coaching. These are great for brand building and community building.

Consider having Fitness VIP Days. You can have 3- to 8-hour 1:1 or group VIP days and take people grocery shopping, take them through a workout, create their training and nutrition programs with them, and do a Q&A session. These are great for charging higher premiums because the value is insane.

You can also offer 30-Minute Online Fitness Audits. You can say you are auditing and breaking down people's training and nutrition programs. Get them on a call to educate them and then sell them into your Hybrid Training coaching. These are great low-barrier-to-entry points and lead generation.

Challenges are also popular. You can run challenges for 14–30 days. Deliver a ton of value within training and nutrition. You can either charge for a challenge and try to sell them into your Hybrid Training coaching at the same time, or you can charge a low price for entry, and at the end of the challenge, you can sell them into your Hybrid Training coaching. These are great low-barrier-to-entry points and lead generation. These are great for brand building and community building too.

Writing for Pay is another strategy we recommend. You can write for online or local print markets. This can help build your name, get you new followers, and give you some extra income.

You can build training software like Trainerize or Coach Catalyst. You can build nutrition software like Avatar Nutrition or Eat This Much. You can also come up with an app that has all your training, nutrition, cardio, templates and content in there, so clients can access them. The creativity is endless with these!

One of the most underrated money-making opportunities in the fitness industry that we want you to take seriously going forward is building your personal brand. This leads to speaking engagements, appearances, affiliate and joint venture opportunities, collaborations, sponsorships, and influencer marketing. It opens many money-making doors.

Inner Circle student Juan Salgado built out a 4-week weight loss course (see it here https://dynamicduotraining.clickfunnels.com/4weekcourse) as his lower ticket offer and to have more of an automated program.

Is your mind blown by all the money-making opportunities? There really is no excuse not to go out there, make money, and become a dynamic fit pro.

Pricing and Packaging

Do you see all the money-making opportunities…crazy, isn't it?

Let's talk pricing now. In our opinion, there isn't a step-by-step process to teaching pricing. There's so much context in each offer, program, etc. However, we found that following these three steps can be a useful way to understand your pricing and packing.

Step 1 -

Teaching the value ladder concept, which we learned from Russell Brunson, has helped our Inner Circle students tremendously with pricing and packaging. Look closely at the value ladder and determine where your product or service fits.

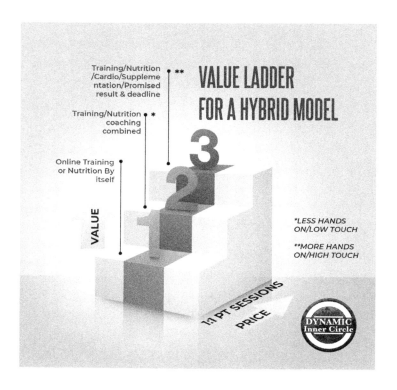

Ladder Step 1

Notice that we're only offering training or nutrition coaching by itself. There is value in it, but not a ton of value, so we can't charge too high of a premium for this. We might charge $99 a month for this.

Ladder Step 2

We now offer training and nutrition coaching, so the value is going up, thus bringing the price up. Tack on some "low touch/less hands-on" approach, where you don't check in with them more than once a week, and the value goes up more. We might charge $199 a month for this.

Ladder Step 3

With this step, we are offering individualized training, nutrition, custom cardio protocol, a tailored supplementation program to complement the diet, and a specific result with a deadline. Additionally, it is more hands-on and with higher touch, which means checking in two times a week. Now the value is through the roof! We might charge $1999 for this 8–12 week transformation package.

You can get more creative with stacking on the value with your offers, such as:
- Daily tips
- Phone or video calls
- Guided movement screens via Skype or Zoom
- Guided assessment via Skype or Zoom
- Daily motivational messages
- Mindset training/lifestyle coaching
- Private Facebook group
- Exclusive WhatsApp text and audio group

- Sleep and stress tips
- Weekly or monthly injury prevention, mobility, foam rolling, stretching tips
- Weekly or monthly healthy recipes and meal ideas

Value, value, value = increasing the price and making more money!

Step 2 -

After you understand the value ladder concept, the next step is to whiteboard your packages and offers. We can't give you a "perfect" package or offer. It all depends on how you want to serve your clients, your niche, your specialty, and methods as a coach. The best advice we can give after a decade of experience and working with hundreds of Fit Pros is to make it simple for your prospect clients. Only give them two options to choose from. Think of a package or offer that has more value in it where you can charge more and then a package or offer that is more affordable.

Step 3 -

After you understand the value ladder concept and have your packages and offers ready to go, it's vital that you know how much you charge for your time. There isn't a magic formula, but a rule of thumb we like to use is:

1) Start with your hourly rate for private sessions. For example, you charge $80 per session, then start with that as to how much your time is worth per hour.

2) Depending on your package and offer based on the value ladder, estimate how many hours it will take to create the program, answer questions, client check-ins, phone calls, etc. For example, say in a 12-week training and nutrition program with check-ins once per week,

building the initial program, making changes to it, and a monthly video call, this adds up to approximately 15 hours total for the 12 weeks, so multiply 15 x $80 = $1200.

3) Play with that $1200 price range and allow monthly payments, or give them pay in full-discounted options, bi-monthly payments, etc.

4) When doing the hybrid training model and pricing, it can get tricky. Refer back to Chapter 3 and pick the model you want first. Then play with this framework for your pricing and packaging:

Framework: Have two separate pricings. One for your in-person sessions (all depends on how many times they come in per week/bi-monthly/monthly) and one for your online packages/offers.

Example:
- 80/20 Hybrid Training Model
- Your client comes in twice per week for 60-minute private sessions
- Your normal rate for 60-minute privates is $100 a session
- $100 x 2= $200
- Since 80% of this is online training, multiply $200 x .80 = $160. This is how much you charge per month for the online program by itself.
- Then you charge them $200 per week for two private sessions per week = $800
- $800 + $160 = $960 per month for an 80/20 Hybrid Training Model. Not bad for one client!

Keep in mind this is just an example and framework that we found has worked for our Inner Circle students. A lot of variables can play into this, but use the value ladder, your time, and this framework as a guide, and it will help tremendously.

This is why we love this four-step process and value ladder concept. We go deep into this with our Inner Circle students during our VIP days because there is no one-size-fits-all solution to offer regarding your services, prices, and packages. It all depends on your niche, the problems you solve, your specialty and method, your credibility and experience, and how much you charge for your time.

Fit Pro to Dynamic Fit Pro Tips

Don't make the mistake we made by creating too many money-making opportunities right off the bat. Pick one core offer and stabilize it, optimize it, and then expand it.

Have fun when coming up with your prices, packages, and offers. The worst thing you can do is copy other people for the sake of it. Be creative, know your value and worth as a coach, and don't be afraid to be different and unique with it all. Test, test, and test some more!

Please fill in the blank:

I'm going to Rise as a Fit Pro because

Chapter 7
LTVC, Customer Experience, Referrals, and Social Proof

"Treat people the way you want to be treated. Talk to people the way you want to be talked to. Respect is earned, not given."
—Hussein Nishah

Now that you have established whether you want to do In-Person PT, Online PT, or the cream of the crop, create a Hybrid Training Model of both, you have seen the money-making opportunities and have a better idea of how to price your packages. You are in a great position no matter what. You should be in an even better position since you have your story down, know your WHY, have a clear vision, identified your niche, and know your specialty as a Fit Pro to stand out amongst all the others.

You are ready for the good stuff! This will really take you to the next level and keep you in the game for a very long time as a Fit Pro!

Lifelong Valued Customers

Customer service, creating relationships, creating awesome experiences, and getting your clients results will help you create lifetime valued customers. This is something we teach heavily to our students in our Dynamic Inner Circle Program. They know we mean business when it comes to customer service, experience, and retention.

With that said, we have four "go-to" ways to create a lifetime valued customer and create an experience for them.

1) 3X Your Customer Service

A shitty attitude, thinking you know it all, having an ego, giving short answers, not wanting to communicate via video or audio, holding yourself on a pedestal, favoring certain clients, jeopardizing people's health, and trying to make a quick buck will put you out of this game very fast and give you the reputation you deserve!

At the end of the day, put yourself in your client's shoes and give them what they pay for. They are putting their health and trust in you to deliver, educate, and change their lives. Customer service should be at the forefront of your business and business values to continue to stabilize, optimize, and expand your business.

You should be honored when a client chooses you to coach them. Don't ever take it for granted because there are other talented coaches who treat people right by giving exceptional customer service, and they will take your place in a heartbeat.

Treat your clients the way you would want to be treated. Exceed their expectations and shower them with Ritz-Carlton-like customer service.

2) Create Relationships with Your Clients

One of the best parts of being a fitness coach is the opportunity to build long-lasting relationships and friendships with your clients. The key to fully earning your clients' trust and having them let down their guard is to get them to TRUST YOU.

The way you earn trust is by taking a general interest in who they are as people. Here are some questions you should be asking your clients:

- What do they do on the weekends?
- What do they do for fun, what are their hobbies?
- Do they have kids, a significant other? Remember their names.

The list goes on in terms of ways to build a relationship. We promise if you do this, your clients will rave about you, refer you, look forward to updates, and most importantly, drum roll, please... They will TRUST YOU and get better results in their fitness journey.

Take a general interest, start asking more questions, and learn to listen to your clients. Even create a spreadsheet with all these questions as columns and keep tabs.

3) Create an Amazing Experience for Your Clients

Giving your clients a memorable coaching experience is so important when it comes to retaining your clients! Just ask yourself this question, "What would I likely recommend?"

Being genuinely cared about and showered with Ritz-Carlton-like experience so you can walk away as a raving fan, or just another number and hardly any communication to where you are left with a lot of disappointment?

I'm pretty sure it's option one.

Listen more, talk less! Don't be that coach that is multi-tasking, checking their phone, or not paying attention when communicating with clients. As soon as this happens, you slowly miss small details from your clients. They will notice this and move on to another coach who will listen.

Here are some tips to help you focus more on your client:

- Put your phone on silent.
- Take off all distracting notifications on your phone.
- Close all distracting tabs on your laptop.
- Take notes during the update to make sure you answer everything.

The art of effective listening is essential to clear communication, and clear communication is necessary for management success. We promise you if you become a better listener, you will gain more respect, improve relationships, and be a better leader.

It's very simple, give your clients the experience they deserve. The following are some suggestions of ways you can give your clients an amazing and memorable experience working with you:

- Give your clients a gift. It's incredible how far a small gift can go in terms of clients showing their appreciation. They may even share that gift on their social media accounts, which leads to more eyeballs for you, thus potential new clients.
- Write down their birthdays on a spreadsheet and send them a handwritten card in the mail. We kid you not, this is such a game-changer in terms of creating an awesome experience.
- Have amazing systems in place, such as your sign-up process, program delivery, support, and check-in process, which should all be done via video to make it more personable.
- Be accessible to your clients. There is no excuse with all the different forms of social media, video, audio, and more. Don't be that coach who is too busy for them.

4) Getting Your Clients Results Leads to Social Proof and Referrals

At the end of the day, results are everything and speak to your expertise and work. A client's main objective coming to you for coaching is for you to deliver results. No ifs, ands, or buts about it! Make sure you are evaluating each client and tailoring their fitness programs to their specific needs and goals. Don't half-ass their programs and check-ins. Check your attitude before responding to clients. Always put your clients in a position to succeed. This will lead to some awesome client testimonials for you to share on your site or social media to bring in more clients.

Make sure you clearly understand their goals and desires. Put them in a feasible position to be able to execute the plan you have for them. Work your ass off to get them to the end destination they want and need.

Make sure you are collecting videos or written testimonials to build up your social proof as a Fit Pro. These are like gold and can be shared on social media, landing pages, and websites to showcase your awesome work as a Fit Pro! This is also great for lead generation.

If you are getting your clients results, giving them an amazing experience, and building a great relationship, guess what? Referrals will be coming to you left and right! Free marketing for you! This is how you scale your coaching business and build an empire. Please don't ever be afraid to ask your clients for referrals if you are doing a great job. Your clients want to help you.

You have to take pride in being a fitness coach, business owner, educator, and leader. Most importantly, make integrity the top priority, along with customer service, building relationships, creating experiences, and getting your awesome clients the results they deserve and pay you for.

When we coach our Dynamic Inner Circle students who want to build and scale their coaching businesses, it always starts with these principles and foundations. This is how you stand out from the rest of the Fit Pros.

Take your reputation seriously and leave a legacy behind with your fitness coaching talents and you will create a ton of wealth and have a thriving business for the long haul.

Fit Pro to Dynamic Fit Pro Tips

CUSTOMER SERVICE, CREATING RELATIONSHIPS, CREATING AWESOME EXPERIENCES AND GETTING YOUR CLIENTS RESULTS WILL HELP YOU CREATE LIFETIME VALUED CUSTOMERS. (We had to put this in CAPS)

Make sure you are collecting testimonials to build up your social proof. Ask your clients for referrals. Go the extra mile to establish a great relationship with them.

Please fill in the blank:

I'm going to Rise as a Fit Pro because

_____

Chapter 8
Sales and Marketing

"The lifeblood of every business is leads and customers."
—Dan Kennedy

Before we break down Marketing and Sales individually, we teach our Inner Circle students to become a fitness marketer first and a fitness coach second. Some of the best and wealthiest Fit Pros out there have a fitness marketer mindset first because they know without having marketing skills they aren't going to get people in their doors to see their coaching skills. How are they going to get people to know who they are online if they can't market themselves?

Reframe your mindset to become a fitness marketer first, so your clients can know who you are and get a chance to experience the awesome coach that you are.

Next up is sales. As Fit Pros, we're not taught to sell. We are taught sales is sleazy, too aggressive, and desperate.

One of our mentors, Mike Zellar, said in our podcast interview, "Selling at its highest level is serving." *(See his podcast interviews here https://www.liveadynamiclifestyle.com/podcast/how-to-look-for-an-influential-mastermind-and-build-meaningful-relationships-with-mike-zeller/)*

Read that a couple of times and let it sink in. Because once we heard that and really let it absorb, we went off to serve, serve, and serve some more!

As a Fit Pro, you have to reframe your mindset around sales and understand that it's just serving at the end of the day. You are a dynamic fit pro with a great skill set and a great solution to people's pain and problems, so why would you not want to serve them?

However, you have to be good at being a fitness marketer first because without the marketing skillset, you won't get opportunities to sell. Once you get good at being a fitness marketer, you then need to become good at selling and closing deals. Let's dig into it all!

Becoming a Fitness Marketer

Just to quickly have you understand the difference between Marketing and Advertising:

Marketing is the umbrella, the ultimate game plan and message to get your services/product out there.

Advertising is under the umbrella. This is where strategies to get your plan and message out come into play.

For example, with the Hybrid Training Model, with marketing, you'd mind map or whiteboard different strategies and plans to get your brand, message, and services out, such as Facebook, Instagram, YouTube, referral system, or a strategy to cross-promote your PT services with businesses within a five to ten mile radius that have your clients.

With advertisements for online training, you can do paid ads on Facebook and Instagram and test different videos, pics, different copy, and offers. With YouTube, you can run a three-part video series with a call to action at the end and target channels that have your clients. For example, you can do a three-part video series on "How to Eat the Foods You Love Without Feeling Deprived" and target big YouTube channels, such as Food Network or channels that come up with the highest view count or subs with keywords like "clean eating."

With advertisements for in-person personal training, you can get brochures made or cool infographic flyers to leave around local businesses or offer a crazy promotion for the workers at the local business to get them in the gym and personal train with you and refer you.

Always remember not to put all your eggs in one basket; something we teach in our *Netflix of Fitness Business Program* is to hustle outside of social media for both in-person and online training to really capitalize on building your Hybrid Training Model.

Now to simplify marketing because it could get too complicated and make you say, "Ahhh, forget this!" We like to explain it in an analogy:

Marketing basics are like having the basics of fitness. If you build the foundation and get the fundamentals down, the more advanced and pro-level stuff works that much better. Trust us, we made a lot of mistakes thinking we could just do the advanced marketing stuff and lost a lot of money.

Beginner Fitness Marketer

- Step 1 - Have a nice, high-resolution logo made on fiver.com or upwork.com
- Step 2 - Have a professional email set up on wix.com, hubspot.com, or zoho.com. A lot of people will use Gmail, and it's fine to use to update clients, but spend the $10 a month to have a professional email where prospects can contact you and get a clear impression that it is a legitimate business.
- Step 3 - Get a phone number for your business on burnerapp.com, sideline.com, skipio.com or Google. This number will eventually go on your site. It's great to have a business number to text people, so you don't have to give out your real number. Plus, having a business number just makes you look more professional and legit.

Intermediate Fitness Marketer

- Step 1 - Make sure all your social media handles are the same on Facebook, Instagram, YouTube, LinkedIn, etc. Also, make sure to clean up your bios and social media handles so that they look professional, clean, and represent your brand and message. Think of these as your resumes to showcase your skills and how you solve people's problems.
- Step 2 - Create a landing page or coaching application funnel with all your services, testimonials, credibility, your story and why, and how you solve people's specific problems with your specific method or specialty. We don't recommend full websites. It's just not needed at this stage and can get confusing for your prospects. One-page landing pages and coaching application funnels are clear, straightforward, and

easier to get people down your funnel. They have worked amazingly well for our Inner Circle students.

- Step 3 - Create a free email marketing platform through mailchimp.com so you can link it to your landing page or coaching application funnel and give away a free ebook, video series, or guide to capture a name, email, and phone number. Always remember social media is rented land, but your email list is land you own.

Advanced Fitness Marketer

- Step 1 - Audio, Writing or Video? We say all three! However, pick one that you are comfortable with and double down on that. Make it a goal to get good at the others.
  - o Audio - you can do podcasting, or sound cloud audio nuggets on training and nutrition.
  - o Writing - you can start a blog, write to your email list, or post mini-blogs on Facebook and Instagram.
  - o Video - start a YouTube channel, go live on Facebook and Instagram, or use Instagram stories. "A pic is worth 1,000 words, but a video is worth 1,000 pics."- Mike Arce
- Step 2 - Where do you want to showcase your content? A lot of it depends on your customer and where you can grab their attention. So, consider Facebook since billions of people are on it. Consider Instagram because it has six neighborhoods (stories, stand-alone posts, IGTV, IG live, DMs, and highlight reels). YouTube is a monster in itself, being the second largest search engine behind Google. Then there are others to test out, such as LinkedIn, Pinterest, Snapchat, or you can even start a blog. Pick one or two places where you

feel comfortable and confident enough to get your message out and showcase your content.

- Step 3 - Create Valuable, Intentional, and Shareable (VIS) content on social media. It's quality over quantity. Make sure it's *valuable* content with a high-resolution picture or catchy video that has actionable steps and takeaways for your followers. Make sure it's *intentional*, meaning you're speaking to your ideal customer, not the whole world. Make sure your messaging is congruent with your customers. It should also be *shareable*. If you create valuable and intentional content, by default, people will share your content, tag, comment, like, and engage with it.

- Step 4 - Understand the Know, Like, Trust concept - Once you have created VIS content on social media, you must master the KLT (Know Like Trust) concept. How do you get a stranger to become a friend to become a buyer? Get them to know you, like you, and then trust you. You have to get the know part down first through VIS content or else you can't warm them up to trust you and eventually buy from you. Video marketing is king and the fastest way to get people to know, like, and trust you.

Pro Fitness Marketer

- *For in-person PTs who are renting space or training at a small boutique gym.* Look into these sites to build up your local celebrity status: Yelp.com, yellowpages.com, citysearch.com, yext.com, and moz.com

- *Paid ads* - Consider Facebook ads, Instagram stories, swipe up ads or regular IG pic/video ads, YouTube ads, Google AdWords campaigns, LinkedIn ads, and even advertising on the Waze app.

- *Other advanced strategies* - Email marketing campaigns, text message campaigns, chatbots through Facebook, influencer marketing campaigns, or paid ads to your landing page, coaching application funnel, blog or podcast.

We know this is a lot, but if you really understand the Four-Tier Concept to Becoming a Fitness Marketer above and don't skip steps, you will build your Hybrid Training Model the right way and have much more success with marketing and advertising to generate more leads.

Becoming a Fitness Server

Notice how we said "Fitness Server" instead of "Salesman or Saleswoman"? That is because selling at its highest level is serving. You are in the industry to serve people with your unique gifts and talents through your coaching services.

Now that you understand becoming a fitness marketer first, and you are able to get people into your gym or get customers online, you must master selling and closing deals.

If you can master the Advanced Fitness Marketer steps above, then you are able to give value in advance through your content. You have to deliver value in advance before asking for the sale. Out deliver people on content and you will win because they will get to know, like, and trust you. That's when you have a moral obligation to serve them and come in and sell your awesome coaching services.

We've been doing sales for a decade now, have personally learned from top salesman like Cole Hatter, Mark Lack, and Tai Lopez, and we have learned from a distance from people like Grant Cardone (see our podcast interview with him here - https://tinyurl.com/yemh6y7z), Dan Lok, and Mike Arce through watching videos, reading books, and listening to audio for thousands of hours.

After all of this experience and knowledge, we're still not master salesmen. Sales is a numbers game, and not even Grant Cardone and his sales team close 100% of their deals. You have to be okay with that. But you can't be okay with not getting better. You have to keep enhancing this skill of sales, being a continuous student, role-playing with people and your team, keep learning to handle objections, learn from others, and attend courses or workshops. Always keep your pipeline full of prospective leads that come from being a fitness marketer first.

We wish there were a step-by-step process we could give you to be a better Fitness Server, but we can tell you that the ten-step framework we've come up with has helped us close hundreds of leads that have led to hundreds of thousands of dollars over the past decade. Our Inner Circle students are learning to master it as well to create more income, influence, impact, and independence.

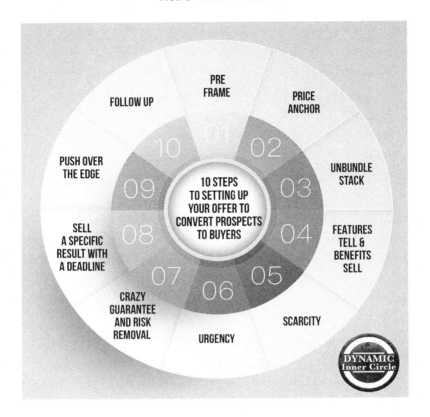

Step 1- **Preframe: The $75,000 Fee**

In Robert Cialdini's book *Pre-Suasion*, he tells the story of a colleague who was having dinner with a prospect. After his standard presentation and just before declaring his $75,000 fee, he joked, "As you can tell, I'm not going to be able to charge you a million dollars for this." The client looked up from the written proposal he was studying and said, "Well, I can agree on that!" The meeting proceeded without a single subsequent reference to compensation and ended with a signed contract.

This tactic of mentioning an admittedly unrealistic price tag for a service or product doesn't always win the business (too many other factors are involved for that), but it almost always eliminates challenges to the charges.

Incorporate a tactic like the example above in your sales process by preframing with a higher dollar amount. Additionally, paint a picture of how the consultation is going to go and what is going to happen. This reduces anxiety and stress and puts the prospect at ease, thus lowering their resistance walls to purchase.

Hybrid Training Model Examples:
In-Person: Preframe when setting up your appointment over the phone before having them come into the gym. Say things like:

- "Did you hear about us (the gym you train at) on the local news story on best kettlebell training?"
- "Have you heard about our trainers from all the articles they've been featured in?"

Also, have them fill out a mini questionnaire online or when they get to the consultation. Ask questions that dig into their pain points such as:

- How many days per week are you able to commit to working out?
- Are you in good general condition?
- What injuries do you have that might impede your progress?
- What's your main motivation for working out?

You're essentially preframing the authority and social proof of the gym you train out of and pre-selling them by figuring out their pain points and motives to want to work with you.

Online Training: There are two main pre-frames we like to do within online training consultations. A) Have them fill out a pre-application and ask questions like:

- Where are you currently at with your training and nutrition right now? (or What is your current level of fitness?)
- Briefly describe your current fitness and nutrition plan: How often do you work out? Are you following a specific nutrition plan?
- What do you feel is your biggest obstacle in reaching your health and fitness goals right now?
- Why will solving this problem make a difference in your life? (Details, please.)

B) Right when you get on the Zoom or Skype call, ask them if they saw your testimonials page and which one they most related to.

You're A) pre-selling them on figuring out their goals and pain points to sell them hope and confidence and B) preframing your social proof and specialty as an online coach by asking if they've seen your testimonials.

Step 2 - **Price Anchor**

This is a great pricing strategy that we dove into in Chapter 6, but essentially you want to have two options for your clients to choose from when getting ready to close the deal. One of those options needs to be very high. That psychologically makes the second option become a no-brainer.

Hybrid Training Model Examples:

In-Person: This depends on if you are selling personal training packages or if you have a reoccurring model where they get X amount of sessions per week. Let's use the selling PT packages as an example:

> *Selling PT packages: Single Session- $75/hour,*
> *Option A) 50 Sessions- $3,500*
> *Option B) 20 sessions- $1,399*

*Do you see how option A is the price anchor? It's a big number to invest. By having your single session rate there as well, it price anchors option B to be a no-brainer. By giving them only two options to choose from, it's an easier buying decision because they are choosing A or B.

Online Training: We recommend something similar to in-person training. Just present two options. Option A) Higher ticket transformation package that is $2,000 for 12 weeks or Option B) $200–400 per month depending on what you deliver or create a package that is $500–999 for 8–12 weeks *Option A will price anchor option B and you will sell more of these.

Step 3 - **Unbundle Stack**
This is where you take everything you do (refer to the value ladder in Chapter 6) and unbundle it. Stack your offer so people can psychologically see all the value they get in their investment.

Hybrid Training Model Examples:

Works for both in-person training and online in a very similar fashion. Which would you rather invest in? An 8-week boot camp with for 60-minute sessions twice per week

OR

an 8-week best-shape-for-summer pro-level boot camp, with the following:
- Two 60-minute sessions per week
- Personalized meal plan
- Personalized grocery list
- Online accountability group
- Accountability coach
- Once per month group meet-up
- Daily motivational text messages

With the second, you are unbundling everything you offer to sell the prospect.

Step 4 - **Features Tell and Benefits Sell**
This is where you really want to sell the benefits of your program to the prospect. What is in it for them? What are the benefits of them investing?

Hybrid Training Model Examples:
Works for both in-person training and online training in a very similar fashion.

Features that Tell:
- Training program
- Cardio protocol
- Nutrition program

These features are boring, dull, and just *tell...*

Now check out how to sell the benefits of these features:

- Custom-built training programs, so you can build muscle mass and strength.
- Individualized nutrition program, so you can eat the food you like and not feel deprived.
- Fun and challenging weekly cardio protocol to burn extra calories, so you won't dread doing boring cardio on a treadmill.

Sell them the benefits!

Step 5 - **Scarcity**
This is where you will explain in your proposal and consultation that there is a limited supply, as in, "We only have X spots left." This creates a "you snooze you lose" type of mindset for the prospect.

Hybrid Training Model Examples:
In-Person: Tell them there are only three spots left in your private training sessions, so they should grab their spot today. "Make sure we add your name before it fills up!"

Online Training: Tell them that you only have two coaching spots available for your high ticket program since you want to cap out at five total people, and spots are filling up fast.
*Be ethical and don't lie about the amount of spots that are open; clients will sniff that out and lose trust in you.

Step 6 - **Urgency**
This is similar to scarcity but more along the lines of "time is almost up," "door will be closing soon," or "we won't offer this again until…"

Hybrid Training Model Examples:
In-Person: Tell them your challenge or program starts on Monday, and there are only a couple more days to sign up before closing registration.

*Online Training: Tell them your online group transformation program that starts in a few days, and you're not sure if you will offer it again any time soon. *Again, be ethical and don't lie about the amount of time left to start or sign up.*

Step 7 - **Crazy Guarantee and Risk Removal**

We are big believers in offering a crazy guarantee within your programs and services so long as you back it up. Think about it, you are a badass coach with crazy skills, so why would you not put your money where your mouth is and guarantee them results? Another great tactic is to offer a risk removal. Just think about when you are looking to invest in something; you always feel better knowing there is a risk removal. Phrases like "money back in 30 days" or "results guaranteed" put you at ease.

Hybrid Training Model Examples:

In-Person: Guarantee a specific result with your client, and mention if they don't like the results, you will give them their money back or additional free sessions.

Online Training: Guarantee a specific result with your program, and mention if they don't like their results, you will mail them a handwritten check with their money refunded.
nine out of ten times, clients won't ask for their money back as long as you deliver a massive customer experience, build a relationship with them, and get them results.

Step 8 - **Sell a Specific Result with a Deadline**

Make sure to refer back to Chapter 2 for more details on this, but in a nutshell, if you tie in a specific promise, a specific result, and a deadline, you can charge more because this becomes a transformation package. The specific promise and result is tied in with an emotional attachment and specific pain, and the deadline creates urgency within the program.

Hybrid Training Model Examples:
Works for both in-person training and online training in a very similar fashion.
*Create a program where you can insert a specific **result** (lose 20 pounds or slip into that sexy black cocktail dress) with a **deadline** (in 10 weeks or in 30 days).*

Step 9 - **Push Over Edge**

We all need a little push over the edge to invest in something. This is where bonuses work great. Think about some cool and unique bonuses to offer your prospects if you get any price objections or resistance on the close.

Hybrid Training Model Examples:
Works for both in-person training and online training in a very similar fashion.
Bonus ideas:

- *Easy-to-follow cardio protocol*
- *My top ten mouth-watering, healthy recipes*
- *Four- to eight-week do-it-yourself program*
- *PDFs, templates, video series, extra phone calls*

Step 10 - **Follow Up**

The magic really is in the follow-up because you aren't going to immediately close 100% of your sales. So, the key is to follow up and continue the KLT (Know Like Trust) game.

Hybrid Training Model Examples:
Works for both in-person training and online training in a very similar fashion.

It's vital that you create a Customer Relationship Management (CRM) system to keep track of potential leads, current clients, and past clients. We recommend starting this by using a simple excel spreadsheet like this here (https://tinyurl.com/yzpdrrrc). Then get fancier with time and use CRM tools, such as Infusionsoft, Pipedrive, or Hub Spot. Once you have your spreadsheet of leads, current clients, and past clients, you must nurture these leads by checking in with them, following up, and ending them with value.

Fit Pro to Dynamic Fit Pro Tips

Create a spreadsheet or Word doc. On the first page or tab, create a checklist with all four levels (Beginners, Intermediate, Advanced, Pro) and start checking off all the items that need to be done to get you from a beginner fitness marketer to advanced fitness marketer. Create clear tasks that need to be done with deadlines to move the needle forward.

Be in a seller's mindset every day. As Grant Cardone says, "Sell or Be Sold." Every morning for 15–30 minutes, listen, read or watch sales content to learn new tips to test your sales process and get you in the seller's mindset to close more deals and become wealthier.

Please fill in the blank:

I'm going to Rise as a Fit Pro because

_____

Chapter 9
Implementing the
P.A.L.M.S. Method

"Nobody cares what you did yesterday. What have you done today to better yourself?"
—David Goggins

You have made it near the end here, and we salute you for hanging with us! However, we are still not done yet, fellow Fit Pro. This chapter is one of the more important ones to really make your business come together. As the old saying goes, "Save the best for last."

You're probably thinking, "What the hell does P.A.L.M.S. stand for?" Once we break down each letter, you will understand and see why implementing this method will really help your business for many years to come.

We like to tell our Inner Circle students when we break down the P.A.L.M.S. Method to think of it as the foundation of a house. When building a house, you need to have a strong foundation so you can build upon it, otherwise, it will not hold up for many years. It will break down from time to time, you will have to put money into it all the time, it will give you a headache, and eventually, you won't want to put any more work into it.

To put it simply, if you don't have a strong foundation for your fitness coaching business, it will not last, it will be a nightmare, it will not grow, and you will want to quit. We don't want that for you, so let's dig into the P.A.L.M.S. Method!

(P) Productivity and Time Management

The "P" stands for Productivity and Time Management. When is the last time you have really stopped and asked yourself, "Am I being as productive and efficient as I possibly can be with my time? Am I managing it well?"

Most of us are not aware of our productivity and time management because, as Fit Pros, we have so much going on and are always putting our clients first. If you can't manage your time effectively to get shit done, you will never move the needle forward in your business and in life. Productivity and time management are very underrated and should be taken very seriously if you are a Fit Pro and business owner.

Something we do with our Inner Circle students is literally whiteboard their entire day-to-day schedules and see where they might be wasting time, not seeing certain time gaps they could use, and more importantly, be more effective, even if it is only one to two hours of working on their businesses.

You would be amazed at how much time we find after doing this exercise. Once our students implement these time blocks, they get shit done in their coaching businesses because there is no excuse not to!

At the end of the day, time is money. We can never buy back time, so why waste it? It's all about figuring out a schedule and time blocks that work for you. There is no way you can build or sustain a business if you are not productive and managing your time wisely. There is always time, and it's up to you as a Fit Pro to make it. The question is how badly do you want it?

(A) Action

The "A" in the P.A.L.M.S Method stands for ACTION! Action cures all fear! Now that you have your productivity and time management under control, you are ready to execute and take action on your business. Taking action is what will really separate you from all the other Fit Pros who are all talk.

At first, taking action can be scary, we get it, and many people don't mention that taking action requires confidence. Many people lack confidence for various reasons, but at some point, if you are serious about building an awesome fitness coaching business and improving in all areas of your life, you have to find the courage to increase your confidence and, more importantly, take action on your dreams and aspirations.

We get tons of ideas from colleagues of ours every day. Ideas are important. We must have ideas to create and improve things, but ideas in themselves are not enough. The idea of getting more business and simplifying processes and procedures is of value only when it is acted upon.

Every day thousands of people bury good ideas because they are afraid to act on them. The worst thing as a business owner is living with that "what if?" or "it might have been a success if only..." So if you have a good idea for your business and your clients, and you're confident it will improve your business, then have the confidence to test it out because it could be a game-changer for your business.

Here are some tips to start taking more action and gain more confidence:

- Surround yourself with like-minded people who take action and play bigger.
- Use words of affirmation to increase your confidence and put them somewhere visual to remind yourself daily.
- Ask yourself this question: "What's the worst that can happen if I fail?"

Use action to cure fear and gain confidence! Otherwise, you will never build a successful fitness coaching business. You will always remain stuck and never grow.

(L) Lifestyle

Boy oh boy, are we huge advocates of lifestyle! We don't have a podcast show named "The Dynamic Lifestyle" for no reason!

Something we really hammer home for our Inner Circle students is the importance of building your business around your ideal lifestyle. What kind of lifestyle do you want to have? How much money does that lifestyle really take to have? What brings you joy and fulfills you every day?

Once you get very clear on this, it's so much easier to build your business around your ideal lifestyle and non-negotiables. We see too many Fit Pros doing the opposite and building a business with zero intention, just for money, and they aren't happy because they don't put their lifestyle and happiness first.

Our mentor, Tai Lopez, of Tailopez.com, once said, "In order to live the Good Life, you have to constantly pay attention and balance out the Four Pillars of Life." Each area of our lives must be treated with the type of respect, love, care and focus that we put in others. If you are not familiar with the Four Pillars of Life, they are as follows:

- Health
- Wealth
- Love
- Happiness

Unfortunately, many people overlook these four pillars. Think about how busy we all get with our days and responsibilities. Work, school, family, kids, stress, gym, the list goes on and on. If you take a second to just look at those Four Pillars of Life above, you will understand that those are the pillars that make life beautiful. If you can say that all of those pillars are fulfilled in your life, you must be living the good life and have nothing to worry about. For the majority of society, this will make or break them when going forward in life, and overlooking some of these pillars can cause a lot of problems.

We were guilty of this ourselves. We never really paid any attention to these pillars of life when starting our fitness coaching business, Dynamic Duo Training. Thinking back on it now, no wonder we were in such a dark place, full of pain, anger, and lost in life when we lost our father and battled adversity. If we had discovered these Four Pillars of Life earlier on and really made the effort to pay attention and improve in each area, we could have been much happier individuals.

If you have dealt with losses in your family, we are sure you can agree with us that health, wealth, love, and happiness are nonexistent for quite some time. We experienced this, and we want to save you from experiencing the same thing. If something bad ever happens in your life, revisit these four pillars as fast as you can and focus on what you can control. Most importantly, consider these four pillars when building your business. Let's look into these four pillars more in-depth now.

Health

Let's face it, without your overall health, you cannot enjoy or master the other pillars of life. Health overrides everything. Think about how many wealthy, intelligent, and successful people there are around the world who do not take care of their overall health. Oftentimes, we get so consumed with what is in front of us that we put our health on the back burner. It doesn't matter if you are a Fit Pro. Something we don't pay attention to as fitness professionals is our mental and emotional health because we always put our clients first, but it shouldn't be that way. You come first and always should. Make sure you are paying attention to your mental and emotional health, or it will come back to bite you.

Wealth

The word wealth means several different things to us: having more money, more power, success, traveling, changing lives, and leaving a legacy. What is your first thought when you see or hear the word wealth? We ask you this question because you should have your own definition of the word wealth. Once you figure out what your definition is, write it out and put it somewhere visible. You can also rate yourself from 1 to 10 for your current wealth and ask yourself, "What choices can I make today to set myself up for long-term financial freedom?"

Let's take a moment and use some of our definitions for wealth that we listed above. Everything we listed is what gets us motivated every day to be the best versions of ourselves and get 1% better all around. One, in particular, traveling, really gets us excited! We love the thought of being able to get up and travel anywhere we want at any point in time. This is wealth to us! Once you find out what you see as wealth, it will help motivate you even more and make you want to attain that goal or dream. Keep in mind, without your health, you cannot enjoy your wealth.

Love

You don't need to talk to someone with a Ph.D. to understand love. Ask your grandma what her definition of love is. We guarantee her answer will make you light up like a Christmas tree. Maybe some of us are not looking to be in love with a significant other right at the moment, but eventually, you might like to experience it and ultimately think it's the key to being happy. Maybe some of us are looking for love within families and friendships first. Everyone is looking for something different when it comes to love; it really comes down to where they are in their life.

We feel the majority of people need to be looking to improve their self-love before anything. Self-love is so overlooked in today's society.

If you were able to give yourself more self-love, ultimately, you would be happier with yourself, and it would be a happier world all around.

It comes down to where you are in life and what you are seeking to improve upon. Sure, the status quo suggests we all need to fall in love and live happily ever after, right? If only it were that simple and linear. Love starts with being comfortable with who you are, being vulnerable, knowing your identity, and knowing what your calling is in life. You have to start with self-love and know you are wonderful and loveable inside. Not because others think so. Self-worth comes from only one place, yourself! If you cannot love yourself, how can you expect to fall in love with someone else or show others love? Ask yourself, "How can I give more and allow myself to be vulnerable with the people who really care about me?"

Happiness

The last and final pillar of life, ladies and gentlemen, is happiness! If you want to be happy, you have to teach your old brain some new tricks and start thinking more optimistically! We live in a world where one little thing can shift our mindsets and completely ruin our train of thought, mood, and day. For instance, many people use their social media to express how "happy" they are or they compare themselves to other people's glamorous lives. This is complete bullshit! There are so many distractions and misleading things in today's society. You can't get caught up in all that drama out there. Think more positive thoughts for yourself first, then worry about another person's happiness.

When you train your brain to think more positive thoughts, you are more likely to form positive habits, which then leads you to more positive results. We know it is not easy to always think positive. Let's face it, life is full of ups and downs. Often during tough down times in life, we find ourselves stuck in a downward "negative-thought spiral." All too quickly, we go from thinking "this one thing sucks" to "my whole day sucks" to "my whole world sucks"!

True happiness is about the thoughts you have, what you have, and who you have in your life. We choose whether or not to enjoy what happens to us. If you take responsibility for everything in your life (including your happiness), you'll find yourself enjoying the little moments and things that truly matter in life.

Balancing All Four Pillars of Life

John Maxwell said, "There's nothing like staring reality in the face to make a person recognize the need for change. Change alone doesn't bring growth, but you cannot have growth without change."

Now that you have an understanding of building a business around your ideal lifestyle and all the Four Pillars of Life, it's time to take action and make some changes in each Pillar of Life. Nobody has this all figured out. These pillars should constantly be changing as time goes on, as you get wiser, or as different life instances happen. The most important thing is to make a change in each area. Do not get complacent with your Pillars of Life. We know we will honor our word and continue to grow in each area; make sure to keep your word and do the same.

(M) Mindset

Next up in the P.A.L.M.S. Method is the "M," which stands for Mindset. Mindset is something that was never taught in school and for a lot of us not in our upbringings, so it's our responsibility to consistently work and build our mindsets each day.

Mindset is probably 80 percent of the battle as a Fit Pro and Entrepreneur. Along your journey, you will see why constantly working on your mindset will separate you from all the other Fit Pros out there to play bigger, stay in the game longer, and never quit!

In our Dynamic Inner Circle program, we take a lot of pride in mindset and really help our students condition their mindsets all around such as:

- Acquiring a CEO Mindset
- Building a Growth Mindset
- Becoming Emotionally, Mentally, and Spiritually Relentless
- A Positive Money Mindset
- A Committed Mindset

Developing a Relentless and CEO Mindset

Being relentless is a state of mind that can give you the strength to achieve, to survive, to overcome, and to be strong when others are not. It means craving the end result so intensely that the work becomes irrelevant in everything you do in life. In the movie *Lone Survivor*, Mark Wahlberg says, "You are always in the fight, never quit." That is the type of relentless mindset you need in order to survive in this world, your business, and get ahead. Nothing will ever be given to you, nor will anyone ever feel sorry for you; remember this statement, and you will be one step ahead of everyone else.

As a Fit Pro, you are the leader and commander each and every day. Every day, you have to program your mind to play offense and always be in attack mode. Use this A.I.A. acronym each day:

- Awareness: Be aware of everything going on in your life; self-awareness is key.
- Intention: Be intentional with your actions and with what you want to accomplish.
- Action: You are either growing or dying each day, so if you aren't taking action, you aren't growing.

Take care of yourself every morning with a morning routine to set the tone for each day. This is how a CEO Mindset is developed. Remember, you are in control of your emotions, actions, and choices you make. Control what you can and don't stress what you cannot.

Don't Live in Fear, Acquire a Growth Mindset Instead

Something we have observed over the last five years is that society lives in fear. At the end of the day, fear is what holds us all back from what we really want to do, right? Think about how many people follow the path of least resistance, are comfortable with their current state, and fear failing. This is something we have paid very close attention to in ourselves, family members, friends, significant others, and clients and students we have coached.

Not to mention, many people grew up seeing their parents live in fear while the school system tells them to play it safe. Growing up, we are taught to play it safe and follow the rules. We were never taught how to take action, lead, or the importance of our mental, emotional, and spiritual health. That advice can be harmful when you start letting fear rule your life. Social rules and fears prevent you from achieving your dreams. Arnold Schwarzenegger once said, "Rules are meant to be broken, just don't break the law." It's normal to feel fear; fear should get your blood pumping full of excitement because you do not know what the outcome is going to be.

In a nutshell, many of us were conditioned to have a fixed mindset, not a growth mindset. A fixed mindset is where you are conditioned to not want to learn, grow, seek advice, and apply it. On the contrary, a growth mindset is always seeking knowledge, being a sponge to absorb new concepts, and continuously being a student in life. You have to reframe your mind to want to grow each day. You do this by overcoming fear, being a student, being around a supportive and positive environment, and never quitting.

In the book *Relentless*, Tim Grover states:

"Most people are the lion in the cage. Safe, tame, predictable, waiting for something to happen. But for humans, the cage isn't made of glass and steel bars; it's made of bad advice and low self-esteem and bullshit rules and tortured thinking about what you can't do or what you're supposed to do. It's molded around you by a lifetime of overthinking and overanalyzing and worrying about what could go wrong. Stay in the cage long enough, you forget those basic instincts."

Grover continues to point out how we put limits on ourselves because of fear. "When you feel fear, you recoil and put up a wall to protect yourself. Is there really a wall there? No, but you act as if there were. Now you can't go forward because of the wall. Put your hand through it, there's nothing there, you can walk straight through it. But if you stay behind that imaginary wall, you fail." This is 100 percent accurate, and we will be the first ones to tell you we have put up our fair share of walls along our journey. If you have a wall up currently, kick that wall down and take what's yours!

Developing Mental and Emotional Toughness

We all have thousands of choices to make in our lives each and every day. The choices we make are what ultimately dictate our health, wealth, love, and happiness. When we lost our father in 2004, lost our grandmother, and lost part of our mom, we had the choice to either give up on life or keep pushing forward. We had our moments where we got into trouble with the law. We could have kept going down that path, but we didn't. We remembered where we came from and how our parents raised us. We knew we had too much potential to offer the world, rather than throw it all away.

We didn't have a secret formula for mental toughness when we were going through all these tragedies; we developed mental toughness along the way by making mistakes and learning from them. At some point, you have to adapt to every situation you are in. What we can tell you is that we mastered three things that really helped us mentally and emotionally get through challenging times.

1. Make the Right Choice
   Don't put all your eggs in one basket. Take your time to identify all the pros and cons of each choice you have, trust your instincts, and refer to your core values.

2. Manage Your Stress
   Stress is stress, and it is not going anywhere anytime soon. Learn to manage your stress on a daily basis, and do not ever let it overtake you and your emotions. Try breathing

techniques, walks, yoga, podcasts, words of affirmation, and sometimes just chill out.

3. Create Emotional Resiliency
    We are all emotional human beings, and our emotions can get the best of us. It's ok to cry and let those sorrows out, just don't let them override what you are focused on. Learn to master your emotions.

Cultivating a relentless, emotionally resilient, CEO mindset is not an overnight task. Vision, focus, discipline, belief in self, humility, and the pursuit of greatness are all the products of developed emotional intelligence, a fine art that requires a lot of practice. Nothing great happens overnight; be patient and develop that relentless mindset that is inside of you. You were put on this earth to be great and make an impact!

Having a Positive Money Mindset

This is an area we wish we could have worked on a lot earlier as Fit Pros and entrepreneurs. We were never taught about money by our parents. Our parents were very frugal, and that carried over to our money mindset as well. It wasn't until joining elite high-level masterminds, hiring coaches, reading books on money, and being around people playing bigger that we learned to recondition our money mindset to play bigger and become wealthier Fit Pros! Now we get to teach these practices to our Inner Circle students because, as Fit Pros, many have scarcity mindsets. So did we, so we feel your pain. At some point, if you want to get to the next level, you have to get out of that scarcity mindset, form a better relationship with money, and believe that the universe will honor all your hard work and good intentions.

One of the biggest obstacles to making money is not lack of good ideas, opportunities, or time, or that we're too slovenly or stupid. It's that we refuse to give ourselves permission to become rich. Again, this most likely comes from our upbringing.

A healthy desire for wealth is not greed; it's a desire for life. Repeat that a few more times.

Money is just the messenger. It's what you do with it and how you think, feel and speak about it that gives it a personality. And depending on the personality you give it, you're either going to want to surround yourself with it or stay away.

Giving and receiving money is an energetic exchange between people. Your job is to consciously get your frequency in alignment with the money you desire to manifest and open yourself to receiving it. As a Fit Pro, you have a gift to offer people that will change their life. Be confident about that, and don't apologize for charging a premium.

If you are afraid to charge a higher premium for your coaching, then get clear on the value of the product or service you're offering. Be excited and grateful instead of weird and apologetic about receiving money for it. Have total faith that money is coming your way because you have good intentions to help others.

Money is currency, and currency is energy. Desperation mode doesn't help this, and we see too many Fit Pros in this mode. Don't be this Fit Pro.

Money is never a bad thing; it's what you do with it that matters. Today, start creating a positive relationship with money and reframe your mindset to look at it as you have every desire to be wealthy.

Developing a Committed Mindset

If not now, then when?

If not this, then what?

We remember being at Tai Lopez's mansion in Beverly Hills for one of his mastermind meetups. It was midnight, and he was still teaching. He told us, "It's better to be impatiently patient as opposed to patiently impatient."

What he meant was it is okay to be a bit impatient when starting your business because you took action, you're hungry, you got started, and you made a commitment. This can then lead to being busy and slowly building the business over time.

As opposed to being patient, where people wait and wait and wait for the "perfect timing" because they're so patient. This leads to paralysis by over-analysis, always looking for excuses, procrastination, and no commitment. When they finally pull the trigger to start their business, all that patience has been counterproductive and leads to impatience when growing the business, leading to mistakes, money lost, and eventually quitting.

So be impatiently patient, and get started today. There is no perfect time to do it, so make the commitment!

(S) Systems, Structure, Strategy, and Support

The last and final letter in the P.A.L.M.S. Method is "S" or we can even call them "The 4 Ss"

Each and every one of these are key when building and growing your fitness coaching business because they keep your business flowing and generating income.

Systems

Imagine if your coaching business had no systems in place. That would be a nightmare. When it comes to putting systems and processes in place, think of the following:

- Set up Trainerize
- Set up templates and spreadsheets
- Liability and agreement forms
- Proposals
- Payments
- Delivery and onboarding process
- Check-in processes
- Sales process
- Exercise library
- Exit process/testimonials
- Referral program

The bulk of your fitness coaching business will be in your Systems and Processes, and this will make your life easy once these are all implemented.

Structure

If you look back at Chapter 2 where we talked about our "10 Step Online Training Business Basic Processes," this is considered structure and can be used for In-Person Training and a Hybrid Training Model. Have a step-by-step structured process in your fitness coaching business that you or your team can follow. Just think about this—when you go into the gym, in order to get optimal results, your workouts need some sort of structure. The same goes for business. You need to have structure; don't just wing it.

Strategy

Be extremely strategic and intentional with every move you are making in your fitness coaching business. Some examples of what it means to be strategic are:

- Lead generation/capturing leads
- Social media content
- Creating a better experience for your clients
- Referral processes
- Thinking outside the box
- Research and development
- Hustling outside of social media (meet-up groups, partnering with local businesses)
- How can I delegate this task?
- How can I make this process automated?
- How can I make my business better?
- How can I eventually grow?

Support

When looking at support, we want you to think of how your fitness coaching business will support your clients. What's the structure and process behind your customer support? Some tips to think about for customer support are:

- How accessible will you be as a coach?
- What forms of contact (phone, email, WhatsApp, social media) will you use?
- Will you have particular office hours to answer check-ins or questions?
- How long will it take you to get back to them?

Really think about the structure of your customer support and stand by it at all times because customer service and experience are what will separate you from all the other Fit Pros out there.

Fit Pro to Dynamic Fit Pro Tips

Implement the P.A.L.M.S. Method in your fitness coaching business. If any of the acronyms do not resonate with your business, then remove them.

Please fill in the blank:

I'm going to Rise as a Fit Pro because

_____

Chapter 10
Playing the Long Game as a Fit Pro

"We only get to play this game one time. We have one life."
—Gary Vee

What does playing the long game really mean? If you stop and think about it, we all can live a very long life as humans. The thing is, many people play small, never take chances, live with that "what if," or simply live a life of mediocrity so in their eyes, life is short. But it really isn't a short life if you do the complete opposite and play bigger in your life and look back and say, "Damn! What an awesome ride that was!"

So when playing the long game as a Fit Pro and in business, the question is, are you willing to go all-in and lay it all on the table? How long can you last in the game?

This game of being a business owner and entrepreneur can be very, very long and rough, so you really have to buy into the mindset that we talked about earlier and develop thick skin as a Fit Pro.

We remember when we interviewed our friend Alex Hormozi, the CEO and Founder of Gym Launch. He talked about playing the game of business at a FINITE or INFINITE level, and it made perfect sense.

So our question for you is—Are you playing the FINITE game or the INFINITE game as a Fit Pro?

Let us break this down for you.

When playing the Finite Game, you have the mindset that the game of business ends at some point, and you will have a massive payout day.

When playing the Infinite Game, you don't let the game of business end. You figure out a way to keep it going by scaling it, helping more people, and understanding that it is part of who you are and your lifestyle.

If you are serious about building an amazing Fitness Coaching Business, you have to buy into playing the game of business at the INFINITE LEVEL.

There is no way to win in business. The goal is to figure out how to keep the game going. This will help you shift your perspective and allow you to understand your market place better and make better business decisions

We have seen so many other fitness professionals throw in the towel and quit, make foolish mistakes, get too greedy, never hire mentors or surround themselves with others playing bigger, and most importantly, don't see the bigger picture or play the long game in their business.

This is something we see very clearly. Thank God for having mentors, a powerful network, and always being students to the game and working on ourselves.

So, you really have to ask yourself, how bad do I want this? How far am I willing to go on this journey, and how long can I last in this game? Once you answer those questions and are certain about continuing on, you will be ready to go to battle each and every day as a Fit Pro, and you will be one hell of a coach.

You will also see the bigger picture and not rush things. Be patient, continue to lead with value, and enjoy the journey as a business owner. Playing the long game is the key to success!

Conclusion

We know how you're feeling right now—overwhelmed, excited, nervous...

Remember, we spent hundreds of thousands of dollars through coaches, masterminds, and mentors to acquire this knowledge and information. We made over $250,000 worth of mistakes (I blame 90% on Eric), and you know what the best part is? You don't have to make the same mistakes.

We hope that we gained your trust throughout this book and that this can be a massive short cut for you to becoming a dynamic fit pro through the Hybrid Training Model.

We selfishly enjoyed writing this book for you here in Palm Springs because we have a huge vision to pay it forward to Fit Pros. Remember that being a Fit Pro is one of the best careers to get into because you get to change people's lives through health and fitness, and you are giving them back hope and confidence.

With that said, always remember your value and worth. You deserve to be wealthy, monetary wise and however else you define wealth.

We hope you enjoyed this book as much as we enjoyed putting it together for you. It was a lot of work, but it was all a labor of love to be 100% real.

Maybe we've met before, maybe we will cross paths soon, either way, we thank you from the bottom of our hearts for your attention and time to read this book. We hope it served you well. You are a part of the Rise of the Fit Pros tribe now!

Thanks for spending time with us, we will talk soon.

-Chris and Eric Martinez

P.S. Take all nine of your answers to *"I am going to rise as a Fit Pro because"* and put them somewhere visible so you can see them daily, take action, and see how the universe will work in mysterious ways :)

P.S.S. Better yet, share your answers on social media with the following hashtags to show the world you're ready to be a dynamic fit pro!
#ImAHybridTrainer #RiseOfTheFitPros #dynamicfitpro

Afterword

It's Time to Take Things to the Next Level

If you want to create more income, influence, impact, and more independence, and be a dynamic fit pro, then you really should implement the Hybrid Training Model. It's time to start playing bigger in your career and take it to the next level by having an online component and a strong in-person training business as well. Remember that those who trained as independent trainers and had an online component were able to create more income, influence, impact, and independence.

This book provides you with the concepts and steps you need to get started with the Hybrid Training Model. You have everything you need in this book to get going.

At the same time, we know some Fit Pros are serious action takers and are hungry to get to that next level through buying speed. If that's you—looking to get to the next level, become a dynamic fit pro through building the Hybrid Training Model, and accelerating the process, then we invite you to join our Dynamic Inner Circle.

Our Inner Circle family is a community of like-minded, hungry, dynamic fit pros looking to always create more income, influence, impact, and independence.

Do you mind if we leave you with a story from one of our Inner Circle students, Juan Salgado (@the_chosenjuan1), who bought money at a discount?

A year ago, Juan **bought money at a discount...**

I know you're probably like, "Wait up...what do you mean he bought money at a discount?"

A year ago, when he sat in our office for six hours in Santa Monica, California, for a VIP day to break down his plans to do a Hybrid Training Model, he had a scarcity mindset in relation to money. He was already concerned about the six-hour coaching day investment. We could tell by his body language that first hour.

{hit the fast forward button on the remote}
The six-hour coaching day was complete, the eight-week game plan was in fine print, his weekly accountability phone calls were completed, and the biggest asset he built was his coaching application funnel to convert online clients.

{hit the fast forward button on the remote again}
A year later, he's quadrupled his income because he **bought money at a discount.** Here's an example of buying money at a discount: *(read this a couple times to grasp it)*

Juan invested $5,000 for the six-hour coaching day with us.

He walked away with an asset that he now owns (the coaching application funnel), that will yield dividends over time far beyond the initial $5,000 investment.

He ran an ad campaign driving traffic to the coaching application funnel where they bought his online coaching for say $1,000, and he sold to three clients each month, that's $36,000 over the year. Over the next five years, that amortizes to $180,000.

This turns into a discount of $175,000 ($180,000 - $5,000 for the coaching day with us).

This is what intelligent business people like Juan try to accomplish any time they pay for expertise; **buy money at a discount.**

Our question to you is, just how many times would YOU like to buy something for $5,000 that will yield $180,000 over five years?

If you want to accelerate the process as quickly as possible, then we invite you to apply to our VIP Program where you will spend six hours with us here in Los Angeles in our office (or virtually) and then have eight full weeks with us by your side, with our fullest attention on you. Apply here: https://go.dynamicinnercircle.com/vip1

If you aren't 100% sure about our VIP Coaching Day we encourage you to watch 5 Amazing and Powerful Real Life Case studies from some of our talented Inner Circle Fit Pros that are absolutely killing the game. You will also get 5 Tips to Start your Hybrid Model Training Business here http://www.dynamicfitpros.com/hybrid-case-studies35310666

Or maybe you want to start slow, get your hands dirty, and do a lot of the leg work yourself—then we invite you to join our monthly Dynamic Inner Circle Elite. Think of this as the Netflix of Fitness Business, where you will have an exclusive members' area with live trainings from us and experts on sales, marketing, personal branding, social media, money mindset, and how to be a better overall coach. Join here: http://dynamicinnercircle.com/elite

Whichever path you choose to go on, we are excited about your future as a dynamic fit pro.

-Coach Chris and Eric

Learn more and join today at
http://www.dynamicinnercircle.com

About the Authors

Chris and Eric Martinez, also known as the "Dynamic Duo," operate a world-class Online Fitness and Lifestyle Company by the name of "Dynamic Duo Training." Chris and Eric are also business coaches who own "The Dynamic Inner Circle," where they help fitness enthusiasts build and grow their online coaching businesses.

Along with being #1 International Best-Selling authors and speakers, Chris and Eric have built a six-figure online fitness coaching business and have worked with thousands of people online and in person to help them look better, feel better, perform better, and live a dynamic lifestyle through training, nutrition, mindset, personal development, and lifestyle practices.

Chris and Eric have also worked with hundreds of fitness coaches to help them build their online businesses and scale them. After investing in high-level business masterminds groups, elite coaching days with business and marketing coaches, losing $250K in mistakes, and having an online business for the last eight years, Chris and Eric's mission now is to pass on their gifts and expertise to other fitness coaches.

As successful entrepreneurs themselves, Chris and Eric believe that everyone has the right to an abundant lifestyle and the responsibility to help others have the same.

They practice what they preach on a daily basis, and that's to live a dynamic lifestyle, which in their eyes means to keep evolving in life, health, wealth, love, happiness, and to never live a static and complacent lifestyle. Be excited every morning and reach for the stars, you deserve it!

Websites:
https://www.dynamicinnercircle.com/
https://www.dynamicduotraining.com/
https://www.dynamicinnercircle.com/elite
https://www.dynamicfitpros.com/adapt
http://www.dynamicfitpros.com/hybrid-case-studies35310666

The New Era of Fitness Book:
https://go.theneweraoffitness.com/freebook
Email: support@dynamicinnercircle.com
Phone: 213-319-6702
Facebook: https://www.facebook.com/dynamicinnercircle/
Instagram: https://www.instagram.com/chrisandericmartinez/
YouTube: https://www.youtube.com/user/Dynamicduotraining
Podcast: https://www.liveadynamiclifestyle.com/

Printed in Great Britain
by Amazon

48828406R00081